W9-BAI-129

The Salad Lover's Garden

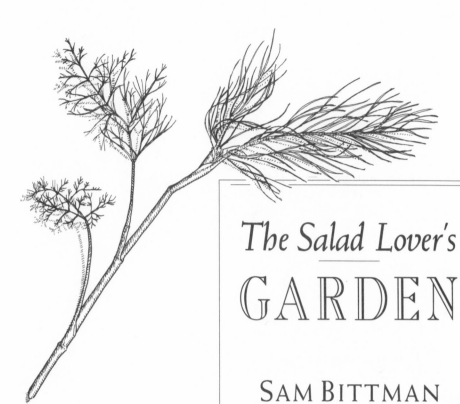

The Salad Lover's
GARDEN

SAM BITTMAN

Illustrations by Elizabeth Barbour
Photography by Dency Kane

DOUBLEDAY
New York   London   Toronto   Sydney   Auckland

For Herman Bittman and Rose Raim

PUBLISHED BY DOUBLEDAY

a division of Bantam Doubleday Dell Publishing Group, Inc.
666 Fifth Avenue, New York, New York 10103

DOUBLEDAY and the portrayal of an anchor with a dolphin
are trademarks of Doubleday,
a division of Bantam Doubleday Dell Publishing Group, Inc.

Book design by Richard Oriolo

Library of Congress Cataloging-in-Publication Data

Bittman, Sam, 1943–
The salad lover's garden / Sam Bittman ; illustrations by
Elizabeth Barbour ; photography by Dency Kane. —1st ed.
        p.   cm.
Includes index.
1. Salad greens.   2. Salad vegetables.   3. Salads.   I. Title.
SB351.S25B58 1992   91-2730
635—dc20   CIP

ISBN 0-385-41414-5

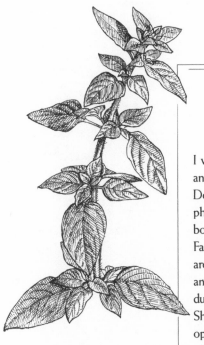

Acknowledgments

I wish to thank Sarah Novak for her research
and good spirits, and Betty Barbour and
Dency Kane, whose illustrations and
photography have made this a truly beautiful
book. Sam and Elizabeth Smith of Caretaker
Farm CSA in Williamstown, Massachusetts,
are always generous with what they know
and what they have, and were especially so
during the final phases of writing this book.
Shepherd Ogden of the Cook's Garden
opened his wonderful gardens for us to take
photographs and provided valuable
information on the extensive varieties of
salad crops he has under cultivation. Also,
Renee Shepherd of Shepherd's Garden Seeds
was kind enough to provide me with the
seeds for my salad garden of 1990. Thank
you to chefs Clayton Hambrick of The
Church Street Cafe in Lenox, Massachusetts,
Jaime D'Oliveira of Angels Restaurant,
Providence, Rhode Island, and Gary Dank of
Chateau Souverain, Geyserville, California.
Thanks to Blantyre, a hotel of the Relais &
Chateaux group; to Berkshire Garden Center;
and to Paul and Margaret Barbour and the
Stockbridge Mission House for letting us in
to see their beautiful gardens. And thanks to
Angela Miller, who smoothed the way.

Contents

1

The Romance
of the Salad Garden

My salad days,

When I was green in judgment, cold in blood,

To say as I said then!

—Antony and Cleopatra

Conjure the spring: Bulbs burst into color, ferns unfurl, young grass pushes up eagerly—everything is new, fresh, and full of promise, including gardeners.

After being pent up all winter I am seized with a furious energy and appetite in early spring. I cannot resist the urge to thrust my hands into the soil, break up clods, pick out stones and roots. I forage hungrily for wild things—dandelion, wild garlic, chicory, fiddleheads, mountain thyme—to toss into a bowl with a little olive oil and lemon, salt and pepper, and then devour. And oh! the delicate blend of those tangy greens—the tender sweetness, the bitter crunch—what flavors could ever compare?

This primordial hunger in early spring for the first tender shoots the earth sends up is, I've come to believe, the instinctive response of a creature reawakening with the world. Alas, spring is a short-lived affair, passing all too quickly. But by tricks and strategies and botanical connivances, we can rely on the salad garden, with its young lettuces and onions, chicories and spinaches and mustards, to re-create for us the mood and feel and appetite of the year's first and tenderest season.

THE SCOPE OF THE SALAD GARDEN

In recent years, millions of health-conscious Americans on the lookout for nutritional, nonfattening food have discovered the salad "meal." Restaurants have responded with an astounding variety of salads with ingredients that used to be far more familiar to Europeans than to Americans. But then, that should come as no surprise; we Americans have long resisted fresh vegetables, whereas in Europe they've always been at the very heart of the cuisines.

But those days are past, as a visit to the produce section of your local supermarkets will demonstrate. You will have to pay a lot, and the stuff may not be so very fresh, but the array of "gourmet" salad vegetables is expanding all the time. You know arugula has hit the mainstream when even a rural IGA has it on prominent display.

The gardeners of America have traditionally been further along than the general public when it comes to expanding taste horizons; even so, it is simply amazing to note the widely expanded offerings of seed catalogs in just the last two or three years. While in the past gardeners scouring American catalogs might find one or two varieties of chicory, now they can find all kinds, from the root chicory that when forced produces the delectable chicons of Belgian endive, to the Verona, Castelfranco, and Treviso varieties of radicchio. There are sweet lettuces of several colors and for all seasons, piquant salad greens from the Orient and Europe, edible flowers, and more!

The salad universe has so enlarged that to accommodate all the cultivars (cultivated varieties) available to us as growers, we'd need gardens the size of a small county. As you will see in Chapters 5 and 6, I have limited the actual number of vegetables and herbs in this book to about forty, with lists of varieties running into the hundreds. And these lists are by no means complete; I have focused only on the half-dozen or so catalogs with the most interesting offerings.

Still, there are foods which you might say are missing—vegetables which you would like to include in your salads, such as peas and beans, beets and kohlrabi, and herbs which you especially like but which do not appear in this book. I suggest that you consult a good general gardening book—such as my own *Seeds: The Ultimate Guide to Growing Vegetables, Herbs & Flowers* (Bantam, 1989), John Seymour's *The Self-sufficient Gardener* (Dolphin Books, 1979), or Dick Raymond's *The Joy of Gardening* (Garden Way, 1981)—for directions on how to grow those crops.

Most salad vegetables are quite simple to grow; others are more challenging in that they require particular growing conditions or special handling techniques. However, even beginning gardeners can enjoy at least some measure of success with salad crops. I hope that my directions will be clear enough so that you can grow whichever salad crops suit your fancy.

Still, finding room for a large assortment will require a sizable plot. If you don't have the space, as few of us do, don't despair. I have put together a sample salad garden that measures just 15 feet by 15 feet. This modest plot will, if conditions permit (the weather can wreak havoc upon the best of plans), produce a surprising assortment, albeit in small quantities, of lovely salad fixings. Herbs, both for chopping into salads and for flavoring dressings and vinegars, can be grown in small pots on the periphery of the garden, as can edible flowers.

SALAD GARDEN DESIGN

For some years, I designed a circular salad garden that was always located in the center of my vegetable garden. All main pathways led to it, so whenever I entered the garden, my gaze was automatically drawn there, as to a glittering gem in the setting of a ring. This year, I decided to replace my cutting garden of annuals with salad crops, but I still managed to design a central circle in the midst of a good deal of rectangularity.

You may choose *not* to have an entire garden devoted to salad plants, and elect instead a certain number of crops, including both the familiar and the experimental, to integrate into your regular summer garden. You could, for example, get several lettuces, a few interesting new greens, some spinach, radishes, and carrots off to a fast start in the spring. Then, as other crops come and go and space makes itself available, you might set in a crop of, say, cress seedlings, or plant a catch crop of cilantro among the corn, or put in a lovely planting of finely curled endive known as frisée (*free*-SAY)—or anything else you see in Chapter 5 that is of interest to you. And the configuration of your salad garden is up to you. Your attention to colors and textures of salad plants will give the garden both variety and beauty.

THE HEALTH BENEFITS OF THE SALAD GARDEN

Salad vegetables contain lots of fiber and no cholesterol, and many are loaded with vitamins and essential minerals. I believe that the healthier the soils in which vegetables are grown, the more powerful is the life force they will impart to the bodies which ingest them. For that reason I follow only organic methods in my gardens, and I urge you to do so as well. For beginning gardeners, that simply means using natural fertilizers such as animal manures, homemade compost, green manures, and a host of other available and naturally occurring soil amendments. Avoid exclusive use of chemical fertilizers, for they are merely plant food and contribute nothing to the long-range health of the soil. (See Chapter 3 for more information on fertilizers.)

Growing plants draw nutrients from the soil—nutrients we must be certain to replace. If we follow the example of nature in building soil, season after season, we will have left our portion of the earth even better than we found it. Details on enriching and improving soil are provided in Chapter 3.

In addition to producing higher-quality produce for us to eat, healthy garden soil will support sturdy plants that more readily withstand attacks from insects and diseases. But even when insect and disease problems do arise, don't be alarmed. There are many things you can do to protect your plants without blasting them with toxic insecticides or fungicides. Such products are designed to control infestation in the short term, but they have long-term negative effects. They routinely damage or even destroy beneficial insects and soil organisms, and they can have residual effects on the final consumers, us humans. Throughout this book I will point out a combination of preventive and nontoxic measures to take if trouble comes.

WHAT, EXACTLY, IS A SALAD?

In all arts there are debates. Food preparation is no exception. Some authorities will argue that the true salad contains *only* greens, and they caution further that combining more than three or four distinct flavors at a sitting will corrupt the palate. Others, including myself, define a salad as virtually any combination of raw vegetables (more on this in a moment) that *please* the individual's palate, whether or not such pleasure conforms to a theoretical gourmet standard. To us, a salad starts with leaf crops but also includes edible flowers, stem vegetables like celery, sweet fennel, broccoli, and cauliflower, and fruiting crops such as tomatoes, peppers, and cucumbers.

Now, to be sure, should the salad plate become an indiscriminate mélange of tastes, the diner will be far less likely to discern and appreciate distinct flavors. But who am I to dictate taste? As for salad dressing, we are told that certain oils, vinegars, and seasonings are more suitable to certain combinations of ingredients than others (e.g., nut oils go well with salads that feature nuts and cheese), and that the oil in a dressing should be in reasonable proportion to the lemon juice or vinegar (i.e., too much oil makes the dressing flat, while too little makes it too acerbic). But in the end, if the dressing you want to use violates all standard salad dressing rules except the most important—what you like—isn't the choice ultimately yours?

Here I must say a few words about salads which make use of cooked ingredients, such as potato salad, the perennial three-bean picnic salad, and composed salads in which vegetables are paired with other principal ingredients such as pasta or rice or fish or fowl or even cheese. They and their principal ingredients are unfortunately outside the scope of this book. However, if these salads pique your curiosity, I can recommend Rosalind Creasy's *Cooking from the Garden* (Sierra, 1989) as an excellent source of information on growing and preparing them.

ENJOY, ENJOY!

Truth satisfies the intellect, it is said, but only passion appeases the heart. Creating a salad garden, that first child of spring, is a thing of the heart and can focus all your passion for nature, for survival, for accomplishment, and for pure sensory pleasure. Do you doubt me? Yes? Then just once stroll out to your salad garden in an early June evening with a basket in hand and browse for the evening meal.

The evening is mild, the light golden. You amble among the growing beds to see what is, at this moment, perfect to eat. Yes, perfect. Look carefully.

What do you choose? A few snippets of red leaf lettuce, a few of green; a small head of buttery Bibb; a handful of still-young chicory, some tangy mustard; a couple of green onions and perhaps just a taste from the bed of salad herbs—lemony French sorrel, and young basil whose heady aroma mingles with the smell of earth and refreshes your senses as you make your way back to the house, renewed.

Now tell me. Is there any place you would *rather* be? Perhaps one. At tableside, as you present your salad creation to the assembled company who will not fail, I guarantee, to see you in a new light altogether.

2

Creating
the Salad Garden

Planning any garden is a matter of dealing with questions of where (the available space), what (the crops you want to plant), and when (an ongoing series of planting and replanting dates). You don't simply plant a salad garden, sit back, and come August or September go out and make your harvest. Your participation in the process is continuous all season long.

WHERE TO PLANT?

If you already have a working garden site—one that you have personally worked before and with which you've been pleased—these next few paragraphs may be of only passing interest to you, for they deal with how to locate or site a garden for optimum success. If, on the other hand, you are trying to decide where to locate a new garden on your property, then by all means read on.

If you've inherited a garden which you will be working for the first time, you might use the following material just to make sure your predecessor had properly sited his or her legacy to you.

Take a look around the grounds. Where would a garden serve you best? You might want it close to the house, handy to the kitchen and to a water supply. Perhaps you'd like to be able to see it from an inside window at which you spend a good deal of time looking out. Or is it important that it be visible along well-traveled paths?

Keep thinking and looking around. But while you do, consider the more crucial criteria—the three S's: soil, sunlight, slope.

Soil

Here's an interesting question: If you haven't gardened on a particular plot of ground before, how do you visually determine the quality of the soil? You need to find soil that's good enough to support a garden. The answer: Examine what is currently growing in the soil. If the prospective garden spot is located on a lawn, ask yourself how green the grass is, whether it's as green as the surrounding grass or the grass elsewhere on the property, and how thickly it is growing.

If you're unprepared to sacrifice lawn for salad, turn to an undeveloped portion of land—a back lot, a field, a side yard that has only grown weeds before. Again, make an inspection. How thick and lush is the growth?

If the grass or weeds are green and healthy-looking, the soil beneath is likely to be rich enough to sustain a garden, particularly after you get through preparing the seedbeds as we will discuss in Chapter 3. But to make sure, you will perhaps like to make a closer visual examination.

With a spade, scalp off a section of weeds or patch of turf and turn up a slice of soil. What does it look like? Is it dark and rich-looking, or is it yellowish? (You want the dark variety, full of humusy topsoil, not depleted subsoil.) Is it moist or is it bone dry? (You want moist.) Press a clod between your thumb and first two fingers. Does it flatten down into a ribbon that holds its shape or does it fall instantly apart? (You want the ribbon, but not so much of a ribbon that a little movement doesn't cause it to crumble apart.)

Is the texture gritty or fine? The grittier the texture, the greater the sand content; the finer the texture, the greater the clay content. Soils that are preponderantly sandy are porous, and water passes through them as it does through a sieve. In such soils, roots have a difficult time taking up enough moisture for good growth, and nutrients are quickly leached from the root zone. Contrarily, clay soils are so finely structured that they tend to compact, making it difficult for air and moisture to penetrate into the root zones of growing plants. Somewhere in between is the ideal soil: a dark crumbly loam.

Soils that are either too sandy to hold moisture or too clayey to allow water in can be dramatically improved when you dig in substantial amounts of organic matter such as peat moss, compost, manure, and leaf mold. So don't fret if your soil doesn't seem perfect at the moment; in Chapter 3 I will show you how to improve most problem soils.

A final consideration in choosing a garden site is to avoid low-lying sites that tend to collect water, for few salad vegetables will do well with their feet in standing water. If you have no choice but to select a boggy plot, there are two steps you can take to improve the situation: (1) Build raised beds, which drain better than flat seedbeds (see pages 30–33 in Chapter 3 for details); or (2) dig a trench all the way around your garden to a minimum depth of 12 inches, lay in a few inches of peastone (which is available from a local contractor or sand and gravel dealer), hook up 4-inch perforated drainage pipe all around, and then fill the ditch with peastone.

If it's still early in the spring, and you actually have the luxury of choosing between several sites, collect a soil sample from each site and send them off for comparative analysis. See pages 35–36 for details.

Sunlight

The next pressing consideration is the availability of sunlight. Most garden crops require a daily minimum of six to eight hours of it, but many leafy crops can do well with less. And while the ideal location for summer gardens is a south-facing site, preferably a hair to the southwest, and pitched a degree or two in that direction, the salad garden will perform nicely with a more easterly exposure as well. That very slight incline toward the path of the sun (the sun crosses the southern sky on the way from the east to the west) increases the exposure by allowing the sunlight to strike the plot closer to the perpendicular. Though such a plot has the virtue of drying out earlier in the spring than others, letting you rush headlong into your gardening passion, it will also be hotter and drier in summer than your leaf crops prefer.

Ideal situations are not always so easy to come by. It might well turn out that the only location you have is one upon which a certain amount of shade falls—say, some morning or midday or late afternoon shadows from nearby trees or buildings. As long as the garden is neither beneath a large tree nor in the continuous shadow of a large building or some other obstruction that bars precious sunlight, you should be okay.

Slope

While a gentle, sunny slope can readily accommodate a garden, a steep slope will present problems for both the garden and the gardener, no matter how plentiful the sunlight. Heavy rains will carry away precious topsoil in a hillside garden unless terraces are built to prevent such erosion. Also, working on an incline is wearying for the gardener.

What can you do if a steep location is all you have? Consider a series of permanent raised beds built into the hillside like a set of steps—higher at the front or downhill edge and lower at the back or uphill side. Plant the area immediately surrounding the beds with some deep-rooted and fast-growing perennial ryegrass to anchor the soil. If the slope is not very steep, you may still choose to garden in raised beds (see Chapter 3), only be sure the beds are built across the slope so that each one catches any runoff from the beds above it.

WHAT TO PLANT?

Seed catalogs are going to be the best source of potential crops for your first garden. Later on, through personal experience and swapping information with other growers, you'll develop favorites, but even then the value of good seed catalogs is that they're always offering new things to try.

Although seed catalogs with beautiful color photographs are welcome in the dark days of winter, some of the best plants I ever grew came from catalogs that you'd consider downright plain. A catalog is of interest to me if it is well written, offers new varieties based on extensive field trials, and shares valuable growing information.

It's important to be able to trust a seed catalog's descriptions. You expect the truth from the seed companies' claims that a particular cultivar (cultivated variety) has unsurpassed flavor, productiveness, and tolerance to disease; that their seeds germinate vigorously; that a plant is hardy for your region. Check the Appendix for listings of some reliable seed companies. My own favorites include Johnny's Selected Seeds, Shepherd's Garden Seeds, W. Atlee Burpee Co., George W. Park Seed Co., the Cook's Garden, and Pinetree Garden Seeds.

As you go through their catalogs, be conscious of the following key characteristics of the varieties you select.

11

Creating the
Salad Garden

Flavor

When it comes to salad crops, taste is what it's all about. Reputable seed companies can be trusted when it comes to the claims they make for their seeds and plants; if a lettuce variety is described in glowing terms such as "Delicious, buttery flavored and blanched heart leaves . . ." go for it. I do.

Date of Maturity

Knowing when a crop will mature and can be harvested makes it possible for you to plan for its successor. Maturity dates are given in days from sowing or transplanting, depending on the variety. As you make your selections, be sure to note the maturity dates on a separate list for future planning. See "The Importance of Succession Planting" later in this chapter.

Yield

This characteristic is normally associated with fruiting plants like to-matoes, cukes, beans, peas, and melons, but it may also apply to spinach and lettuce too (e.g., "prolific bearer"). If high production is one of your goals—and why shouldn't it be, especially in a small garden?—by all means select high-yielding varieties. Beware, how-ever, of any description that touts productivity but suddenly drops all mention of taste. Such descriptions are perhaps intended for market growers who value sheer volume over quality.

Heat Tolerance

Salad vegetables (as I will no doubt mention several times again in the course of this book), especially the greens, prefer the cool weather of spring, early summer, and autumn. The seeds do not germinate well when the soil is hot, and standing plants tend to bolt and go to seed in warm weather. At that point, plant chemistry changes, the plant's energy goes into seed production, and leaves become dwarfed and bitter. As salad crops have become more popular, seed houses have bred heat tolerance into many varieties, which allows us avid salad gardeners the heretofore unknown bonus of sweet and tender greens all summer long. So look carefully for phrases like "heat-resistant," "heat-tolerant," "resists bolting," or "slow-to-bolt," or similar language, and order those cultivars.

Disease Resistance

This is a major consideration. Although plants grown on soil with high humus content rarely suffer major disease outbreaks, inbred disease resistance, when you can get it, is not bad insurance against crop failure. And if a particular variety has such traits, say a spinach that is resistant to powdery mildew, you can be certain the catalog will mention it.

Treated or Untreated Seeds

Emerging seedlings are susceptible to several fungus diseases, most notably the soilborne malady known as "damping-off." If you use a sterile, soilless planting medium when starting seeds indoors, the threat is avoided. Direct-sowing outdoors, however, is another story, and to combat the potential problem, many seed houses used to treat their seed with fungicides. I never liked the idea of a toxic substance on my garden seeds; after all, I began growing my own food to get away from all the chemicals glopped on supermarket produce in the first place. Apparently I wasn't alone, and soon a good number of seed houses began to do away with their fungicidal treatments.

If you have feelings on this issue, either order from catalogs that

Creating the Salad Garden

never treat, or request untreated seeds. While Burpee and numerous other popular seed houses no longer routinely treat their seeds, they do offer packets of the fungicide for gardeners who have ongoing problems with damping-off and other fungus maladies. To prevent damping-off disease, make certain you remove any covering from your seeding flats or containers after germination to allow the air to circulate. It is also a good idea to wipe away any condensed moisture on the underside of the covering.

Miniature Varieties

While most salad vegetables are compact plants, some of our salad bar add-ons like cucumbers and tomatoes like to spread out. If your growing space is limited, check out miniature varieties bred especially for small gardens. Look for phrases such as "bush variety" or "compact bush type" when it comes to cucumbers and squashes, and "determinate" tomato varieties (see page 190 for more details). Also, some "baby" vegetables (Little Gem lettuce and Little Finger and other miniature carrot varieties are examples) are worth checking out for their own sake, irrespective of space considerations. You will find more information on miniature vegetables when we discuss specific crops in Chapters 5 and 6.

THE IMPORTANCE OF SUCCESSION PLANTING

The trick of a successful salad garden is to orchestrate events so a diversity of compatible eatables is ready to be brought to table at almost any moment of the season. Because our delicate salad greens are at their most tender and delicious when they are young, crops should be harvested with appropriate dispatch, and the well-prepared gardener should rework the bed and immediately set out another planting. Creating these successive waves of season-long growth is called succession planting.

The basic concept of succession planting is really quite simple to grasp: Follow one crop with another. A plot of earth is a terrible thing to waste, and succession planting allows you to keep your soil productive all season. The process occasionally calls for some difficult decisions. For example, even in the best-planned garden, there will always be more of something than you know what to do with—say a patch of red romaine lettuce from which you've already harvested ten heads. There are still eight heads left, all of which look quite beautiful and taste magnificent, but you've already eaten lots of romaine, and there's another variety coming in right across the path, and over in your nursery bed you've got a flush of radicchio seedlings just waiting to be transplanted into a vacant spot in the garden.

What to do? Do you let the balance of the romaine sit in the ground taking up valuable space because it's still in its prime? Remember, unless you live in the tropics, the growing season is a limited time, and you must make the most of the time you have if you want to experiment with all those new tastes and textures.

It's not easy to pull up living plants. For years I berated myself for overplanting. But I've come to look at the issue differently of late, reframing the problem so it is no longer a problem, but rather a benefit. First of all, *everyone* plants more than they can use, so let's lay that old breast-beater to rest. Second of all, you can give surplus veggies to friends, who are almost always grateful (except of course if you're trying to unload foot-long zucchini); or, if you live on a farm, you can feed the excess to your chickens or goats or pigs, who will happily recycle it for future use; or you can throw it on your compost pile, which will ditto what the livestock did, only take slightly longer in the process. So stop feeling guilty about uprooting plants that are still producing; you can always find a productive use for them.

The only other thing you will need to become a successful succession sower is a plan, which I will furnish in the next section, "Designing Your Salad Garden."

DESIGNING YOUR SALAD GARDEN

Garden design decisions center around considerations of size, shape, and interior layout.

Size

Size is a "how much" function of overall design: How much space do you have? How much food do you need to grow? How much time and help do you have?

Unless you are growing salad crops on a commercial scale, a salad garden by its very nature is considerably smaller than the average complete summer vegetable garden. Most salad crops are relatively compact plants, and many are picked when young, before they are fully grown. Also, salad ingredients are meant to be served raw and have a limited storage life, so you cannot grow large quantities of them to store for later consumption. Unlike potatoes, which can be kept in primo condition for months after harvest, the peak quality period for most salad vegetables is brief. You can extend these peak periods by refrigeration, but a home fridge is, after all, only so big.

So the object when designing the salad garden is to plan a garden large enough to feed you, your family, and nongardening friends, with a little left over for the livestock or the compost pile. An old standby formula for determining quantity of any particular crop specifies 5 feet of row per person: that is, if your family of five likes spinach, you should plant 25 feet of it. This strategem implies the use of traditional single rows, but as you will soon see, there are more productive ways to plant your garden. Still, it can serve as a basic rule of thumb for deciding how much to plant.

Shape and Layout

The business of food growing has always been a utilitarian undertaking. Farmers laid out their fields in straight lines with ample room between rows for cultivation equipment—first horses and harrows, then tractors with an ever increasing number of attachments.

Most vegetable gardens have traditionally tended to mimic farm fields and are consequently either square or rectangular, with the crops planted in straight, widely spaced rows. There is a satisfying simplicity to the straightness of such a layout, and in large gardens single rows provide a basic convenience for moving essential power equipment in and out. But as I have said, salad gardens are by their nature small affairs, they require less mechanized than personal cultivation, and to my way of thinking they have a generally more ornamental quality about them. Creative layouts can enhance the ornamental aspect of the salad garden.

I do not mean to denigrate rectangles; I use them all the time. Rather, I would urge salad gardeners to be guided by their imagination. What is there to lose? If circular or oval plots are acceptable for flowers, why not for vegetables? If you have the urge, why not plan your salad garden with gracefully curving lines, and pleasing textures and colors in mind, the way flower gardeners plan out *their* borders? I'll grant you that green predominates in the vegetable patch, but my! what a magnificent procession of greens there are when you look closely—to say nothing whatever of the assortment of reds and purples and yellows that have increasingly become a part of the salad landscape. And the textures are just as varied and lovely: Consider the delicate frilled leaves of endive, the softly waved leaf lettuces, the feathery foliage of fennel and dill. Considering the subtle colors and myriad textures of your salad crops when designing your garden can add an extra visual dimension to the scene.

Wide Rows and Raised Beds

Gardeners with small plots and vivid imaginations must take advantage of every possible square foot of growing space. Traditional narrow single rows flanked by wide walkways (as suggested on the backs of many seed packets) will not allow for a diverse garden if space is limited. But there is a solution.

You can turn the formula around and plant intensively. Just make the planting rows wide and the walkways narrow. In the sample salad garden following page 19, you'll see a striking array of salad crops in a 15-foot by 15-foot garden. Rather than narrow rows of individual crops, you'll see wide rows with diverse crops growing together as bed companions.

Instructions for preparing wide rows and building raised beds follow in Chapter 3.

Companion Planting and Intercropping

The practice of intermixing plants in the same planting bed for beneficial effect is called companion planting. Intercropping is a variation calling for planting an entire row or bed of one crop between two rows or beds of another. In either case, the proposed benefits include repelling of harmful insects, enhanced strength from root association, and improved flavor (e.g., savory is supposed to make beans and onions taste better).

Examples of such beneficial pairings are: carrots and peas in the same or nearby beds; onions and peas; parsnips with lettuce; parsnips and potatoes with beans; beets with broccoli; radishes and nasturtiums with cucumbers; marigolds with cabbage family crops (cabbage, broccoli, cauliflower, collards, etc.); and cucumbers, dill, zinnias, and asparagus with tomato, and so forth.

Other companionate groupings have more demonstrably practical applications. Midsummer lettuce planted among tomatoes or corn receives protection from the scalding sun, and winter squash planted amid corn both saves space and discourages marauding raccoons.

You have a world of choices in setting out your garden and only one rule to abide by. In making your garden plan, remember this one: Always plant tall crops like tomatoes or trellised vine crops on the north or east sections of your garden, so they won't cast shade on lower-growing plants. But even this rule, as in the example of lettuce intercropped between tomatoes, is judiciously broken.

With this rule in mind, get out your paper and marking pens and start playing around. Make a list of all the vegetables, herbs, and flowers you'd like to include in the garden, each with a time to maturity beside it. As you find a spot for each in your garden, enter the name, the approximate date when you expect to plant it, the approximate date of harvest, and, in parentheses, the crop that will succeed it, as in the following example: Bloomsdale spinach, 50 days; in, 4/25; out, 6/15; (Radicchio Guilio). Place one check mark next to each primary crop in your list, and two checks next to each succession crop. Once everything in the list is checked off, your plan is complete.

Now that your plan is complete, use it with a certain amount of flexibility. No actual garden of mine ever turned out exactly as I had it planned on paper, and yours probably won't either. Why? Because things happen that you can never anticipate. Suppose a woodchuck gets into the garden and chews all the lettuce plants in a bed down to the nub. Suppose it turns unseasonably hot in early May and your spinach bolts two weeks earlier than you'd expected. What then? Are you going to leave the bed vacant for two weeks waiting to plant a second wave of carrots? No.

In this situation you should think fast, *try* something, become *spontaneous*. Even if it's just to sow a catch crop of radishes, or a seedling crop of cress, or, for lack of anything else, a patch of annual ryegrass you'll turn under three weeks later and for which the earthworms will be forever grateful, plant *something* in that empty space.

Now who would have thought way back during the planning process that a particular lettuce bed was going to be host to a three-week green manure crop? Certainly not I. But these things happen. So don't make yourself crazy over the plan. It's a guide, for goodness' sake, not an architect's blueprint.

Now that we've covered the preliminaries it's time to get out to the garden.

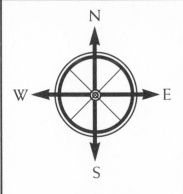

N
W   E
S

15' x 15' = 225 sq. ft.
1/2" = 1'

INTENSIVELY
PLANTED SALAD
GARDEN

- Broccoli di Rapa
- Broccoli
- Cauliflower
- Claytonia
- Radicchio
- Chicory
- Dandelion
- Carrots
- Arugula
- Shungiku
- Cress
- Mesclun
- Mâche
- Celtuce
- Cabbage
- Onions
- Garlic
- Leeks
- Endive
- Escarole
- Radishes
- Celery
- Lettuce

(Items in parentheses
represent succession
crops)

TOMATOES   TOMATO

CHERRY   EARLY PATIO TYPE   MI

W   A   L

Mache (Escarole)	Broccoli (Fall Spinach)
Green and Purple Early Cabbage (Carrots)	Pot Marigolds
Nasturtiums	Mesclun Bed Mild Mix for Baby Greens (Broccoli di Rapa) (Mâche)
Bunching Onions	
Ornamental Kale	Onion Sets for Scallions and Storage
Celtuce Cilantro (Seeding Bed for Fall Lettuce)	Witloof Chicory (Endive)
Leeks	
Celery	
Seeding Bed	

Thyme   Oregano   Dandelion

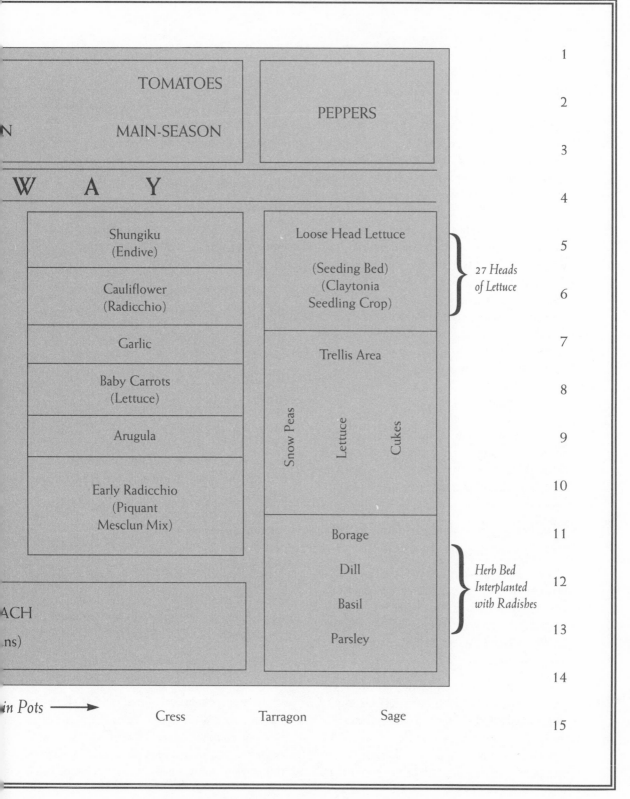

TOMATOES

MAIN-SEASON

N

PEPPERS

W A Y

Shungiku
(Endive)

Cauliflower
(Radicchio)

Garlic

Baby Carrots
(Lettuce)

Arugula

Early Radicchio
(Piquant
Mesclun Mix)

Loose Head Lettuce

(Seeding Bed)
(Claytonia
Seedling Crop)

} *27 Heads
of Lettuce*

Trellis Area

Snow Peas

Lettuce

Cukes

Borage

Dill

Basil

Parsley

} *Herb Bed
Interplanted
with Radishes*

ACH

(...ns)

...in Pots ⟶   Cress   Tarragon   Sage

1
2
3
4
5
6
7
8
9
10
11
12
13
14
15

Container Gardens

If outdoor space is at a premium, you can still enjoy fresh-from-the-soil salad vegetables and herbs from your own patio or balcony mini-garden, which you can create by growing plants in containers. Whether your container garden is a single window box or an array of pots and tubs, the principle is the same: Select a few attractive, fruitful and easy-care plants, generally small-scale, to grow in containers that hold enough soil and water to keep them happy, healthy, and productive on your balcony, roof, courtyard, patio, or windowsill. Unlike the average garden plot, your container garden is infinitely rearrangeable, to suit your mood, the weather, and how many guests you need to fit on your patio.

Containers

Containers come in a variety of materials, styles, and sizes. They need to be strong enough to hold the combined weight of soil, water, and plants. Here are some possibilities:

Terra-cotta: The classic earthenware (clay) vessel in many shapes and sizes.

Terra-cotta look-alikes: Boxes and pots in a variety of shapes and sizes that reproduce the look of terra-cotta in plastic or resin, and won't crack or chip. Includes Enduralon℠, a polyethylene resin developed for outdoor use.

Chinese imports: Glazed stoneware that outlasts terra-cotta in most climates. Urns used for thousand-year eggs have no drainage holes (but could be used as decorative holders for actual planters). Large white-speckled blue-black pots do have drainage.

Concrete: Planters or pedestals cast in Italianate or English shapes with painted finishes; the most popular is natural gray. Try to get pots that are crack- and peel-proof.

Ceramic: Classic glazed pots; choose containers with drainage holes.

Wood, fiberglass: For tubs, large boxes, window boxes in classic shapes. Keep in mind that wood weathers, warps, and rots, while fiberglass isn't supposed to.

Miscellaneous containers: Half a whiskey barrel, hanging pots or baskets, large olive oil tins, wooden crates, bushel baskets (lined, or for holding pots), old bathtubs . . .

Container Garden Accessories

Plant caddies are platforms with wheels, handy for moving large pots into or out of sun or shade, or for rearranging the garden for watering or entertaining. Since the caddies lift the pots off the ground, they also provide for drainage.

Tower gardens are designed for patio, balcony, or even indoor growing. These tiers of redwood slats form a four-sided pyramid of planting space, and the base turns or moves on casters. The concept is ideal for a salad garden. A 4-foot-tall tower creates 46 feet of row on a 2-foot square base; the 2-foot tower has 26 feet of row.

Plants to Grow

Fast-growing, relatively small and shallow-rooted plants are the best bet for container planting, including many varieties of lettuce for harvesting as tender young greens, mature leaves, or full heads. Dwarf versions of traditional salad vegetables—peppers, tomatoes, cucumbers—have been bred for mini-gardens. Sun-loving herbs, such as basil and thyme, also do well. With extra attention to watering, parsley and chives are good choices too. Edible flowers such as nasturtiums add color and taste accents. Here are some selections to consider.

LETTUCE AND GREENS

- *Mixed French lettuces:* Mantilia and Red Oak Leaf can be combined for appealing paired colors, textures, and tastes. Can be harvested as individual leaves or allowed to mature as full-size heads.

- *Italian Green and Red Chard mix:* Plants are productive throughout a long season and are disease-resistant. Young leaves are good in salads and the paired colors are attractive.

- *Windowsill green collection:* Designed at the request of a greengrocer in New York City, this salad mix includes broadleaf cress, curly chervil, arugula, mizuna, white mustard, mâche, claytonia, and lettuce.

- *Container collection:* Try an assortment of short day/early maturing looseleaf lettuce varieties such as Red Salad Bowl, Black-Seeded Simpson, or Green Ice.

TOMATOES

- *Superb Super Bush:* This cultivar produces abundant fruit on 2½- to 3-foot plants; lush foliage keeps plants from sunscald. Grow in 16-inch-diameter pots with small supports.

- *Basket King Hybrid:* Extra early, and excellent for hanging baskets. Its sturdy cas-

cading branches have clusters of tomatoes 1¾ inches across.

CUCUMBERS

- *Salad Bush:* Produces an early crop of 6-inch cukes on dwarf bush vines only 15 inches long. Stands up to both cool and hot conditions.

PEPPERS

- *Cadice Hybrid Bell:* Its large early fruits are both sweet and decorative, turning from shiny green to red on 18-inch bushes.

HERBS

- *Piccolo Italian basil:* Produces intense flavor throughout summer. Each plant is a neat little bush 12 to 14 inches tall, with small leaves.

- *Herb mix:* A nice container collection that includes Piccolo basil, Dukat dill, cilantro (coriander), French thyme, parsley, and chives.

EDIBLE FLOWERS

- *Nasturtiums:* Small, brightly colored flowers will gently mound, fill, and drape in a container without overwhelming. Both leaves and blossoms are edible. Cream and the dwarf Whirlybird are recommended varieties. Needs full sun, or light shade in very hot climates.

Growing Tips

In general, the size of the container determines what can be grown in it. Seedling crops and shallow-rooted herbs need at least 4 inches of soil. Nine to 10 inches of depth and an equal diameter are necessary for larger plants such as tomatoes and peppers. These taller plants may need some kind of staking or other support.

The crucial elements for the success of your container garden are soil, sun, and water in the right proportion.

The right kind of soil: Good garden earth with a generous helping of compost and a handful of gravel and/or peat makes a rich and porous soil. The soil should be changed every two years, usually; plants that use up nutrients quickly, such as tomatoes and peppers, need fresh soil every year and extra feeding during the growing season. In urban areas where soil tends to become acid, you may need to add lime.

The right amount of sun: Six to 8 hours per day is an optimum amount for most container crops. Direct exposure to sun and to wind—on a balcony, for example—can dry out the soil and hamper growth. A vine-covered trellis makes an attractive windbreak and also offers shade in hot weather for spinach, lettuce, and other plants that need shade.

The right amount of water: Your contained plants need more frequent watering than garden-grown cultivars, since containers are susceptible to drying out—the soil is shallow and is more exposed to sun and wind. It's helpful to establish your container gar-

den near a water source. The soil surface can be mulched with stones or gravel; wooden tubs or clay pots can be lined with plastic, if drainage holes are added (see later). Large containers hold moisture longer than small ones, and the soil in plastic or ceramic pots stays moist longer than the soil in wood containers. Soil in stoneware, concrete, and aggregates dries more slowly than in terra-cotta.

Good drainage is essential to prevent waterlogging. Containers must have drainage holes, either in the bottom or an inch above the base on the sides (this way, the box or pot doesn't have to be raised for water to drain). Put a layer of drainage material—stones or pieces of clay pot covered with peat moss, for example—in the bottom of each container before you fill it with soil mix. Windowsill plantings or containers on balconies need drip trays to prevent damage from water draining off onto your favorite carpet or the neighbor's balcony below.

Automatic watering systems are also available. The low-tech version supplies water from a basin or bucket to the soil surface via a wick of absorbent material. The high-tech version uses emitters with variable flow rates to drip water to each container, and can be set on a timer and/or a moisture sensor. You'll want to hide the wicks or lines if their looks don't please you.

3

Getting Into It

In this chapter, we will launch into the sphere of soil preparation, planting techniques, and crop care and maintenance. If you are new to gardening, the information provided here will be extremely helpful, if somewhat detailed. Take it a bit at a time and it will all come clear.

Let's start with tools.

CHOOSING YOUR TOOLS

If you're just starting out as a gardener, you'll need a few tools. You may choose to keep your plot small, about the size of the garden we discussed in Chapter 2—15 feet by 15 feet. Such a garden shouldn't send you shopping for expensive power equipment (see the information on tillers later in the chapter), but even if it did, or if you hired someone to till your garden, you'll still want to have a spade, a spading fork, a hoe, a steel rake, and a few hand tools around for general garden maintenance.

Select these tools the way you buy shoes, with comfort and durability in mind. While price is not necessarily a guarantee of high quality, it's a decent guide, so try to keep away from the low end or you might be buying new tools next year, too.

Finally, make sure each tool comes with a guarantee against breakage under normal wear and tear.

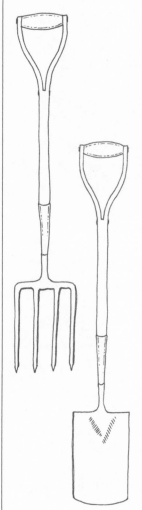

SPADE AND FORK

Spades and Forks

A good spade slices through sod and soil with so little effort that virtually no shock is sent to your arms and lower back—unless, of course, the spade happens to strike a big stone going in. That'll jolt your teeth as well as your back and arms.

The job of the four-tined spading fork is to break up newly spaded ground into medium-size clods. Look for slightly dished forged-steel spade blades and diamond-shaped tines on the fork, smooth D or T grips for easy handling, and handles that are an appropriate length for your height (if you're tall, you don't want to be hunched over a short-handled tool all the time). Don't go much below $20 to $25 each for a decent spade and fork.

Rakes and Hoes

While spades and forks may be classified as digging tools, rakes and hoes are pull-and-push tools. The hoe is used primarily as a weeder and cultivator; it slices off weeds just beneath the soil surface both in garden walkways and within planting rows and beds, and it gently

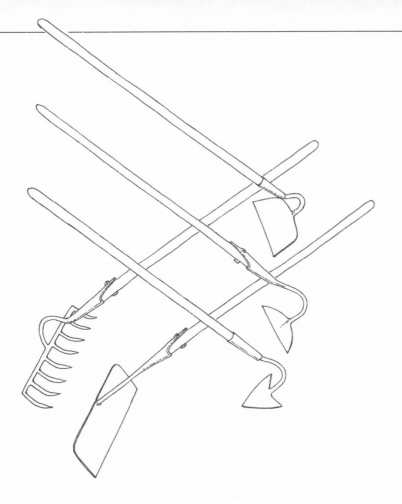

breaks up the soil surface so air and water are allowed easier entry to the root zones of growing plants. There are specialty hoes of all sorts, including very narrow ones for working closely around the stems of plants and a kind of triangular-bladed affair called a Warren hoe which is great for opening deep planting furrows.

I use a rake for a number of key garden chores: to make smooth seedbeds with just the right texture, and to sweep out the rows after weeding, which leaves the garden looking beautiful. Until recently, the rake was my tool of choice for building raised beds (which we will discuss later in this chapter). The tool I use now is featured in the Gardener's Supply catalog as a "raised bed builder." It's a sort of rake-hoe combination, a "hoke." Its blade is solid steel, 4 by 12 inches, and it can move large amounts of soil or mulch or compost beautifully, which makes it much more efficient than a rake for the work of heaping up soil to make either permanent raised beds or ones you rebuild every year.

Swan-neck hoes and rakes are designed to let you work while standing up straight. For gardeners of average height, a long handle in the 60-inch range also helps. The graceful angle of the swan-neck is practical as well as visually pleasing, for it gives you a better "bite" than straight-neck tools, and reduces muscle ache in the bargain. Hoes come with 6- and 9-inch blades, while rakes are a standard 16 inches wide. Swan-neck tools are generally more expensive than straight-neck varieties, but the back-saving is well worth the few extra dollars. Both are in the $20 to $30 range.

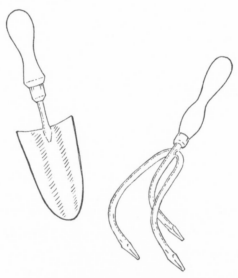

Hand Tools

While long-handled tools are designed to be used with the operator on his or her feet, hand tools are what you use when you're working on your knees. There are scads of hand tools on the market, but all you really need is a trowel for digging planting holes or digging up long-rooted weeds and a kind of claw-fork for weeding and cultivating. Look for high-quality materials and, once again, let comfort be your guide. Decent hand tools range in price from about $8 to $10.

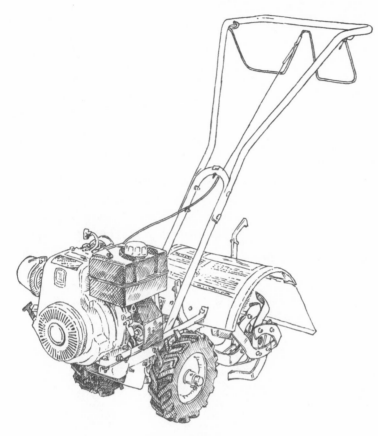

Power Tillers

My vegetable garden is large enough to require the assistance of a gasoline-powered rotary tiller. I've been using the same one since 1977, a 7 horsepower, Troy-Bilt Professional Horse model. It would be a bit oversized for a 15-by-15-foot salad garden, but your gardens will expand one day, and you might rather do the tilling yourself than keep hiring out the work.

Troy-Bilt and Ariens are among the leading brand names, and the only tillers with which I have had personal experience. In your purchasing deliberations, simply forget about front-tine machines. They'll shake you mercilessly from the get-go. Rear-tine tillers, on the other hand, with their drive wheels up front, allow the tines to churn away so smoothly you can manage the machine with one guiding hand even at full throttle.

27

Getting Into It

Starting a New Garden
from Lawn or Grassland

Creating a new garden from a section of lawn or field is no cakewalk, but the rewards are tremendous and are upon you before you know it. The trick is to work systematically, giving yourself a sense of steady progress from one stage to the next. Here's how to do it.

1. Once you've decided how large your plot will be, stake out its corners and string twine from one stake to another.

2. Using the twine as a guide, slice down through the sod with a well-sharpened spade all along the perimeter to the full depth of the blade, about 12 inches.

3. Using the spade as in step 2, divide your plot into subsections no more than 2 feet wide by the length or width of your plot.

4. Now the real labor begins. With your spade, scalp off the turf, one section at a time. You shouldn't have to work much lower than 2 inches beneath the soil surface to accomplish this, but it still requires a good deal of bending. Take care here. Work for a few minutes and straighten up to rest your back muscles.

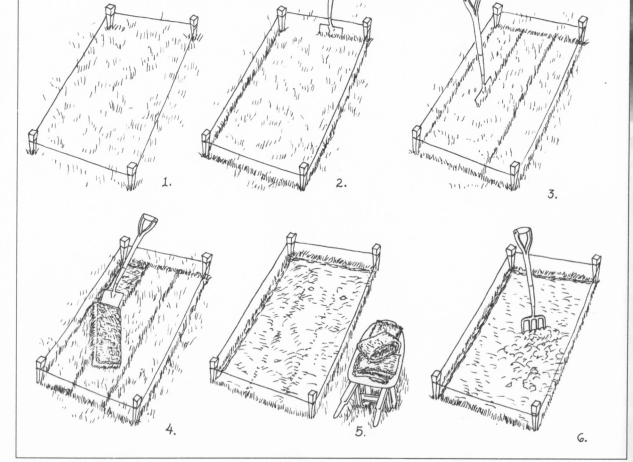

1.

2.

3.

4.

5.

6.

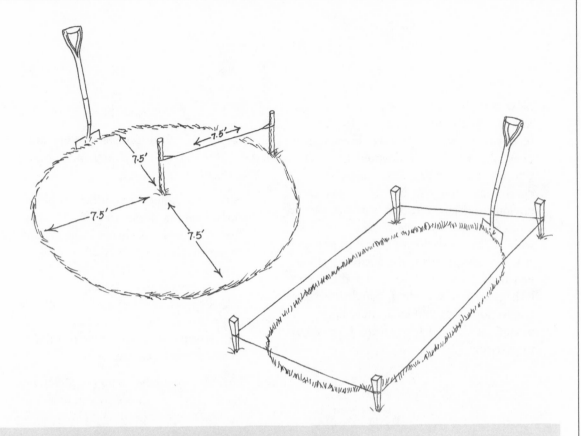

5. You may remove the sod to your present compost pile, or a place where one will shortly be. You can, if you prefer, bury it in your new plot at a depth of 12 inches. This calls for not just turning the soil, as in step 6, but removing it, one section at a time, to create trenches. Lay the sod, grass side down, in each trench and cover with soil from the next section, creating a new trench at the same time. This technique, known as bastard trenching, will be further explained when we take up double-dug beds on page 30.

6. Pushing in your spade or spading fork to the full depth of the blade, turn up as much soil as you can.

7. Break up large clods by banging down with your rake and pulling. Bang and pull until all large clods have been reduced.

If you want a garden with a circular design, make yourself a compass from two pointed sticks and a length of twine equal to one half the circle's ultimate diameter (e.g., for a circle roughly 15 by 15 feet, use a length of twine that measures 7.5 feet). Anchor one stick in what will be the dead center of your circle, and drag the other around the perimeter, making a visible tracing in the lawn. Then follow the directions just described for steps 2 through 7. For an oval shape, stake out a rectangle and round out the corners later by eye.

PREPARING SEEDBEDS
FOR PLANTING

Now that the soil in the garden has been turned, your next step is to prepare seedbeds for actual planting. In small gardens, the more space devoted to actually growing salad vegetables, the more productive the plot will be. That may seem obvious; yet in traditional gardens, where crops are seeded in single rows flanked by wide walkways, a lot of valuable growing space is wasted. Also, the aesthetic of garden beds 2 to 3 feet wide and thick with lush growth is appealing. Single rows are fine for tomatoes, but even there I prefer to mound up the soil for reasons I am about to describe.

Raised Beds

Planting beds raised 6 inches above the ground surface, particularly those prepared in the double-dug fashion (described later), offer rewards beyond beauty. It is axiomatic that the more extensive a plant's root system is, the larger and healthier the plant will be. After all, having more roots expands a plant's ability to take up water and nutrients. In a double-dug bed, the soil is loose and crumbly to a depth of 12 inches or more, enabling the roots of growing plants to expand into it with no obstruction. Raised beds provide better drainage than flat beds, which is especially helpful if you have heavy clay soil. Better drainage also means that your soil dries out more quickly in spring, allowing for earlier planting.

Double-dug Beds

Here are the half-dozen steps in preparing the most productive planting beds a gardener could want.

1. Stake the corners of your bed-to-be and run a string from one to the other. Four feet is as wide as the bed should get, though I like a 3-foot width myself. In any case, don't make the bed so wide you can't reach to its middle from either side. Remember: Essential to this system of gardening is that you never walk on the planting beds. Compacted soil definitely inhibits plant growth.

2. Spread as much manure, preferably aged, onto the surface as you can, a 2-inch covering at the minimum.

3. Open up a trench one spade deep and wide on one end of your bed, and place the soil in a cart or wheelbarrow.

4. Plunge your fork into the subsoil at the bottom of the trench and work it around. Don't turn it; just wiggle the fork until the soil is loosened and elevated a few inches.

5. Dig a second trench right beside the first one, placing the soil from the second trench, with its manure topping, into the bottom of the first. Loosen the subsoil in that trench, too.

6. Dig a third trench, and repeat the process until you've reached the other end of the bed. Empty the soil and manure from the wheelbarrow into the last trench.

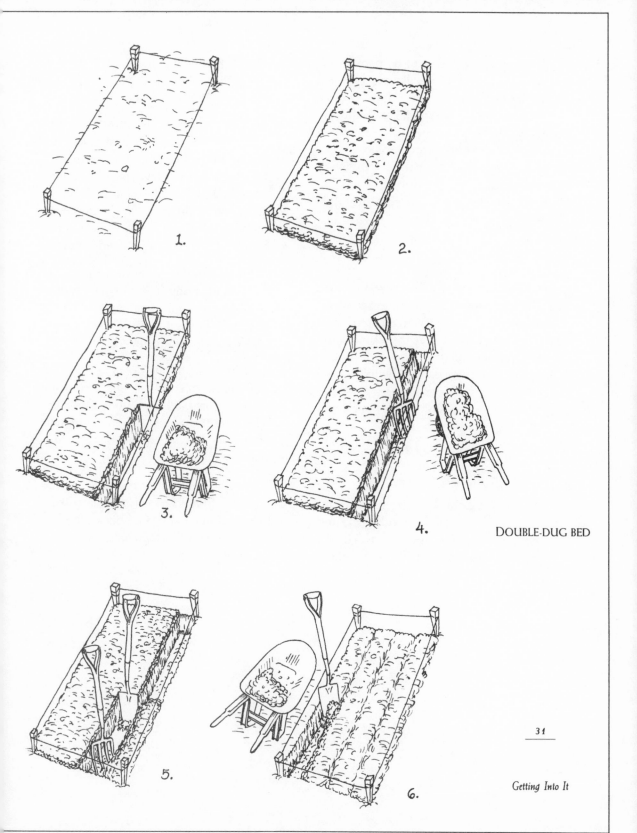

1.

2.

3.

4.

DOUBLE-DUG BED

5.

6.

These beds are meant to be permanent, which means that the walkways between them are permanent, too. Allow enough room in a small garden to walk and cultivate comfortably between the beds, about 16 inches, the width of a garden rake. If your garden is large, make the paths wide enough to allow for a cart or wheelbarrow.

Some intensive gardeners re-dig their beds every year; I believe adding aged manure or compost each season, along with other soil amendments, and forking it all in is more than satisfactory.

In his book *How to Grow More Vegetables*, John Jeavons estimates that to properly dig what he calls a biodynamic/French Intensive bed measuring 5 feet by 20 feet (100 square feet) should take about six hours. That's a lot of work. Alternatively, you might want to consider a raised bed that can be built in a fraction of the time.

Simple Raised Beds

Here is a simpler way to make raised beds.

1. Once your garden has been turned or tilled and raked fairly smooth, stake out the corners of your proposed bed and run a string between them low enough to the ground to give you a good dimensional guide, but high enough to keep out of the way.

2. Standing outside the proposed bed, heap up soil with your rake or raised bed builder *within* the dimensions established by the string. In fact, you will be temporarily drawing the soil away from the strings at a distance of about 6 to 8 inches. At this point, the soil should be heaped into a sort of pyramidal mound.

3. With your rake, flatten out the top of the mound along its entire length until the bed is raised about 3 to 4 inches above the ground and the soil has now headed back toward the strings.

4. Turn the rake upside down and smooth out the surface of the bed, removing stones, roots, and large clods as you go. The smoother the finish, the more uniform your seed germination will ultimately be.

There are no free lunches, so what you gain in time from labor saved you are likely to lose in productivity. Of course, the loss will not be severe, so the compromise may be worth it to you.

The Salad Lover's
GARDEN

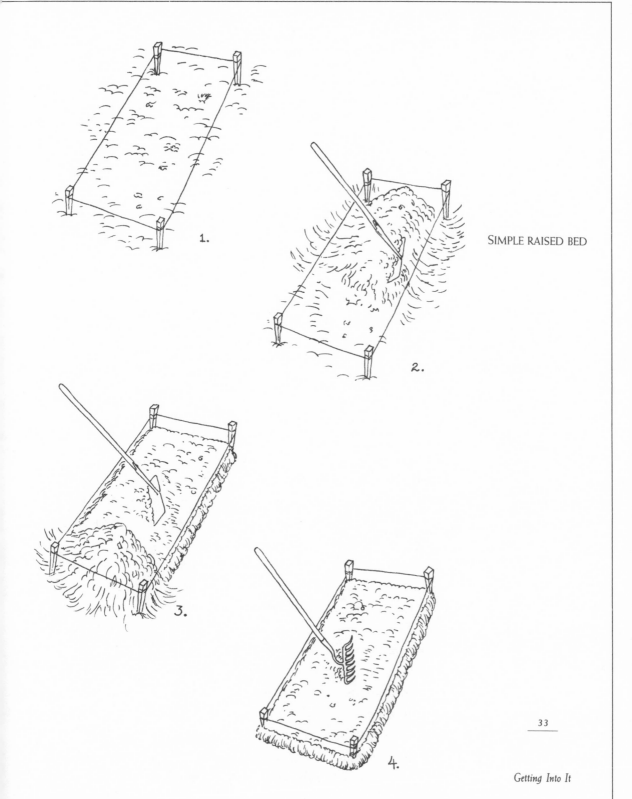

SIMPLE RAISED BED

1.

2.

3.

4.

Getting Into It

Wide Rows

You can avoid raised beds of any kind, if you wish, and still plant an intensive garden. This is accomplished with simple, surface-level wide rows. Wide rows involve less work, and results will be good if the seedbed is well prepared. The only exception could be with your carrots and other root crops such as parsnips, beets, and Witloof chicory, as these vegetables require a good, deep soil to produce well-formed roots. Still, in the salad garden per se we'll only be dealing with carrots and Witloof chicory, and I'll show you later on how to prepare heavy soil for success with these crops.

To prepare a wide row, stake out the corners as for a raised bed and run a string between the stakes. This time, all you need to do is add fertilizer to the tilled soil (see later in the chapter) and rake the bed smooth before planting.

SOIL:
THE FOUNDATION OF LIFE

Most soil, except the most depleted, is teeming with life. It's been estimated that 5 to 10 tons of living matter inhabit every acre of ground: microbes by the untold zillions invisible to the eye, insects, worms, algae, fungi, and other life forms whose job it is to process, or help decompose, the organic matter in the soil.

Organic matter is anything that is or was once alive—plants and animals and insects are all organic matter. In the life cycle that characterizes our planet, all that once lived gets to live again and again, albeit in altered states. This is no attempt to proselytize for the theory of the transmigration of souls; rather, it is natural law.

For example, a goldfinch dies, falls to earth, and before long begins to decompose. Air and water and certain insects work on it. Earthworms drag the remains down into the soil, bit by bit, digesting some of it, leaving some for putrefactive bacteria and other organisms which over time return it to the soil in the form of nutrients available to growing plants, say wild grapevines. The vines produce a staple crop for wild turkeys who, feeding on the grapes, thrive long enough to procreate, which in turn ensures the survival of the species. Who could deny there's a little goldfinch in the next generations of turkeys? The goldfinch (leaf, centipede, tomato, human) lives again.

Decomposed organic matter forms a soil substance called humus. Humus contains nutrients that it releases slowly to growing plants. Humus in the soil acts like a sponge to hold water, and its large particles also help to create necessary air pockets that keep soil from compacting. In addition, it feeds soil organisms, reduces soil temperature in summer, triggers complex chemical exchanges, and much more.

No garden can stay healthy for long without a steady supply of humus. The problem is that, unlike forests and fields where plants live and die and fall to earth along with an almost unlimited supply of leaves, gardens are quickly and quite intentionally stripped of their plants. Gardeners must therefore assume the role of Mother Nature by providing the materials with which humus can be manufactured.

Any organic matter you introduce into your soil will sooner or later become humus. Animal manures, crop residues, weeds, seaweed, peat moss, compost, rotted leaves, and grass clippings are all excellent candidates.

Enriching the Soil

For the most part, salad vegetables taste best when they've grown quickly in cool weather. The richer the soil, the faster your salad crops will grow.

If you're just starting out on a new plot of land, or if you've inherited someone's garden, how do you know how rich the soil is? You have it analyzed, and the results will indicate the levels of the following:

The major nutrients: Nitrogen (N), phosphorus (P), and potassium (K).

The secondary nutrients: Magnesium (Mg), manganese (Mn), and copper (Cu).

Trace elements: Boron (B), calcium (Ca), iron (Fe), molybdenum (Mo), sulphur (S), and zinc (Zn).

Organic matter: Decomposed and partially decomposed plant and animal matter, as discussed earlier.

Soil pH: The acid-alkaline balance which is measured on a 14-point scale, in which 0 to 6.9 is considered acid, 7.0 is neutral, and 7.1 to 14 is alkaline. Most salad crops do best between 6.0 and 7.0, though a wider range of 5.5 to 7.5 is generally acceptable.

The test results will also come with a list of recommendations for improving nutrient content, organic matter, and pH.

But suppose it's midspring already and you can't get it together to send off a soil sample to a testing lab. Does this mean you can't have a successful garden this season? Of course not. Unless your garden soil is like a sandpit or a driveway, you're bound to have some measure of success. Next you'll learn about a host of natural fertilizers and soil conditioners you can buy or make yourself that will not only feed your crops but improve the tilth of your garden soil.

Compost: Fertilizer and Soil Conditioner

When added undigested to the soil, all organic matter will temporarily tie up essential nitrogen, creating the potential for inhibiting plant growth. Therefore, the fastest and most efficient way to build up the humus content of your soil is to let all your available organic matter rot a while before introducing it into the garden. This process is known as composting.

Composting is the gardener's method for speeding up the decomposition of organic material into humus. Essentially, composting is a matter of heaping organic material in a pile and waiting for it to break down. The finished product, when added to the soil, is an excellent fertilizer and conditioner.

Depending on whom you speak to, composting can be either an extremely simple or a rather exacting process. Simplicity or complexity is a function of time. The faster you want your compost to be ready, the more precisely the pile must be layered. When arranged properly and given the necessary air and water, a compost pile will heat up very quickly and turn its contents into usable compost in a matter of six to ten weeks. A so-called "cold" pile, in which materials are tossed on a heap more or less as they make themselves available, could take a year or so to produce usable compost. This kind of compost is also likely to be less rich owing to a natural leaching of nutrients out of the pile.

A COMPOST BIN MADE
OF WOODEN BOARDS

Recipe for Hot Compost

Here's how to make hot compost. First, you will need a container for the organic material. A bin measuring 5 feet by 5 feet by 4 feet in height is just right. Ideally, three bins, each with a compost pile at a different stage of completion, will satisfy all your compost needs. The bin can be made of boards, wire mesh, cinder block, or even hay bales. Because the decomposition process is aerobic, make sure your bin provides plenty of ventilation.

Lay down layers of different materials as follows: First, 6 inches of green matter. This can include fresh weeds, grass clippings, shredded leaves, and kitchen scraps (no meat or bones, however, as these tend to attract unsavory critters to the pile, like rats, and furthermore do not break down readily). Be aware that coarser materials which contain far more carbon than nitrogen—such as fresh leaves, sawdust, wood chips, and fibrous crop residues that have already passed maturity—will take much longer to decompose than materials that are finer textured or contain more nitrogen. Mix these coarser materials with fresh manure or compost and leave them to rot for a while—at least six months—before incorporating them into the compost. Alternatively, you can place them at the very bottom of the pile where they will have the longest time to work.

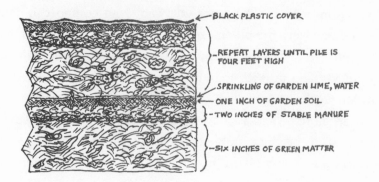

For the second layer use 2 inches of fresh stable manure or, if you have no manure, a sprinkling of other highly nitrogenous material, such as blood meal, fish meal, seaweed meal, or pulverized dog kibble.

On top of the manure, put down 1 inch of garden soil. Among other beneficial things, soil introduces earthworms to the pile, whose presence will hasten decomposition. Follow the soil with a sprinkling of garden lime and a sprinkling of water. (The material should be moist, not sopping wet.)

Repeat this layering until your pile is 4 feet high, and then cover with an old carpet or a sheet of black plastic to keep excessive rainwater from leaching out nutrients. Within a day or two, the pile will start to heat up, and over another several days, it will reach an interior temperature of 160°F, where it will stay for a while. It is at this stage that decomposition happens fastest.

After about four weeks, the temperature will have subsided, and the pile should be turned, bringing untouched materials at the outer fringes of the pile into the center. Water again if the materials seem dry to you and re-cover the pile. In four to six weeks after turning the process should be complete.

Animal Manures

If you live near a working farm, consider yourself fortunate, for you are likely to have a steady supply of fresh manure. Here's a rough analysis of the NPK percentages of the most commonly available manures.

MANURE*	NITROGEN (N)	PHOSPHORUS (P)	POTASSIUM (K)
Chicken	1.1	.9	.5
Cow	.5	.2	.5
Horse	.6	.3	.5
Pigeon	5.8	2.1	1.8
Pig	.6	.5	.4
Rabbit	2.4	1.4	.6
Sheep	.9	.5	.8

*Figures are for fresh manure. NPK percentages are higher when manure is aged.

Other Natural Fertilizers and Soil Conditioners

Many garden supply stores and catalogs offer a bevy of natural fertilizers and soil conditioners from animal, vegetable, and mineral sources. Here's how some of them break down.

	NITROGEN (N)	PHOSPHORUS (P)	POTASSIUM (K)
	(%)	(%)	(%)
Bone meal	2–4	22–25	0
Fish meal	7–8	4–8	0
Horn meal	12–14	2	0
Greensand	0	1.4	4–9
Rock phosphate	0	38–40	4.5
Wood ashes	0	1.5	7
Cottonseed meal	6	3	1
Dried blood	13	1.5	.8

FERTILIZER STARTER KIT

Ecology Action of the Midpeninsula offers in its Bountiful Gardens catalog (see page 196 for this address) what it calls a bio-intensive fertilizer starter kit, the ingredients of which I have used to great benefit in my gardens. This kit is especially helpful for gardeners who don't have access to stable manure. Each fertilizer kit treats 100 square feet of growing space. Contents include

6 pounds of soybean meal (good source of nitrogen)

4 pounds of bone meal (good source of phosporus)

1 pound of kelp meal (good source of potash and valuable trace minerals)

5 pounds of greensand (potash and trace minerals)

Mix contents together in a cart or wheelbarrow, sprinkle a surface layer over your planting beds, and fork into the top 3 or 4 inches of soil. These materials release their nutrients slowly, remaining active in the soil for up to ten years, so don't expect to see results immediately. In fact, it's always a good idea to spread these soil amendments in the fall, if that is convenient.

Lime

ADJUSTING SOIL
PH WITH GROUND
LIMESTONE

So vital is this soil amendment to the health of your garden that I've decided to treat it separately, however briefly. In addition to providing essential calcium to the soil, lime (crushed or dolomitic limestone) performs a number of other important functions. It neutralizes soil acidity, improves the structure of clay soils, helps to preserve nitrogen in the soil, and releases phosphorus and potassium, which tend to be otherwise unavailable to plants growing in acid soil.

Test your soil's pH regularly to see if you need to add lime. As described earlier under "Enriching the Soil," pH is determined according to a 14-point scale. Simple testing kits are available at all garden centers to analyze soil pH. In heavy clay soil, 5 pounds of lime per 100 square feet will raise the pH level by one unit (say, from 6.1 to 6.2). Use half that amount in sandy soils. Liming every three to five years is standard practice. But remember, too much lime can tie up other valuable nutrients in the soil, so test your pH regularly and use lime with caution.

Applying Fertilizers to the Garden

To keep your soil in optimum condition, apply fertilizers directly to the growing beds, even if the beds are not permanent. Compost and aged manures, along with any of the soil amendments listed earlier that provide a balance of nitrogen, phosphorus, potassium, and micronutrients, can be shoveled onto the surface of the bed in the spring, and then forked into the top several inches of soil. It is from this soil zone that most of your plants' roots take their sustenance. John Seymour, from whose *Self-sufficent Gardener* I have learned a great deal, says it is unnecessary to fork in compost or manure; simply heap it onto the surface and the earthworms will draw every bit of it into the soil in due course. Practically speaking, a soil surface of finely crumbled compost also makes an excellent seedbed. Fertilizers may also be

A FEW WORDS ABOUT SYNTHETIC FERTILIZERS

Synthetic fertilizers are in themselves no evil. Rather, it has been the heavy agricultural reliance on these "quick fix" chemicals in place of soil improvement programs which has been responsible for vast stretches of the world's farmland eroding and blowing away like so much sand. Each year the abuse continues as we lose millions of tons of our most productive soils.

You know the story of the farmer who tried to get his mule to do its work without food. Over the weeks, he cut down the mule's ration a little at a time. But just as the mule achieved food freedom, the ungrateful animal up and died.

Synthetic fertilizers are food for plants, not for soil. They supply highly soluble nutrients which generate quick, lush growth (what farmers and gardeners naturally want), but they provide no nourishment for the teeming organisms in the earth, the actual mules of the soil. Soon starved, these largely invisible life forms begin to die in vast numbers. And when they die, the soil structure can no longer be maintained in good shape. The complex community of organisms that exists in a healthy soil exists no more, and the quality of the soil declines. Also, synthetics usually provide more nutrients than plants can use. The excess runs off, seeps into groundwater, and causes pollution.

applied as side- or topdressing during the growing season and again in the fall when the soil is tilled.

TECHNIQUES FOR INTENSIVE PLANTING

Intensive planting, particularly in a small salad garden, offers a variety of advantages—from saving space to increasing overall yield. The techniques described in this section—broadcasting and block planting—also result in planting beds which are beautiful to look at.

Advantages of Intensive Planting

The advantages of intensive planting over traditional single-row gardening are considerable when the beds are both well worked and well fertilized with compost and/or other natural fertilizers. Intensive planting saves space, increases yields, creates a beneficial microclimate for plants, and encourages good root growth.

As I've indicated earlier, you'll save a great deal of space when you plant intensively. In a properly prepared bed measuring 3 by 5 feet (15 square feet) you can plant out twenty-one heads of lettuce (spaced 10 inches apart), whereas the traditional single-row method would allow for only six heads in the same space—fewer than one third the amount. This advantage increases with compact-growing crops like spinach, carrots, onions, garlic, radishes, and mustard.

Because the soil is so fertile, plants can be spaced more closely together. When plants are spaced so their outer leaves just touch when they reach maturity, the leaves create a "shade mulch," which reduces soil temperature (especially helpful for salad greens which prefer cooler conditions), conserves precious moisture (you'll need to water half as much as you must in traditional single-row gardens), and shades out weeds.

Because you never walk on the garden beds, the soil remains loose and uncompacted, enabling plant roots to grow straight down without obstruction. Plants grown in this manner are lush and healthy, with surprisingly long root systems. In single-row gardening, where the soil is prepared only to a depth of 6 to 8 inches, roots are often unable to penetrate the compacted subsoil. Instead of growing downward, they must grow laterally—often under walkways, where competition for air, water, and nutrients is much keener and where damage from treading is virtually unavoidable.

Broadcasting Seed

Once your bed has been fertilized, remove or break up any clods and rake the surface smooth. I use the back of my rake (teeth up instead of down) for this important finishing step. The smoother the bed's surface, the more uniform will be the depth of the seed and, ultimately, the more uniform their germination. So take your time here.

Pour some seeds into the palm of one hand and pinch up a bunch with the thumb and index finger of the opposite hand. With your hand gently waving over the soil at a height of about 2 feet, roll the seeds off your index finger with your thumb. Spread the seed as evenly as you can. This is fairly easy to do with pea seeds or even spinach

43

seeds. But if you're trying to broadcast small seeds like those of lettuce or carrots, you should work closer to the soil, say 6 inches. If the day is windy, place your body between the wind and the bed (if possible) and work as close to the soil as you can.

Gently firm the seeds in place with your hand, the back of a hoe, or even a short board if you have one handy. This is a critical step, as the germination rate increases when seeds are in snug contact with the soil. Next, cover the seeds with fine soil (see listings of individual vegetables in Chapters 5 and 6 for specific seed depths) or finely crumbled compost. Because my soil is clay, and clay tends to crust over after a watering (which makes it difficult sometimes for seedlings to emerge), I often use a light cover of peat moss or sterile planting mix over small seeds. Gently firm again with the back of a hoe, a board, or your hand.

Remember, though it saves time, broadcasting almost invariably results in overseeding. When seedlings emerge, you will have to thin them once, twice, or even three times until the spacing between plants is right. See listings of individual vegetables for spacing distances.

Block Planting

The other seeding method I recommend takes a little more time at the front end, but it will save you the trouble of serious thinning later. It is also the same technique applied for setting out transplants, which we will discuss shortly.

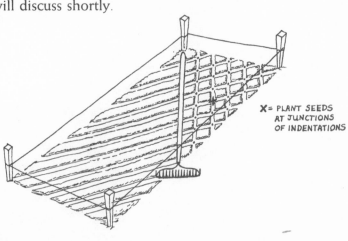

X = PLANT SEEDS AT JUNCTIONS OF INDENTATIONS

The most efficient way to plant a rectangular bed is to sow seeds in a series of fairly closely spaced diagonal rows within the wide row or raised bed (see illustration). This creates a diamond pattern which is repeated over and over again.

Rather than broadcasting seeds, you will sow them one at a time in furrows or "drills" laid out in a crisscrossing diagonal pattern. Think of a lattice-crust apple pie. That's the effect, except your bed's not a circle. Unless of course it is, in which case think of the lattice crust by all means.

Starting from one corner, lay your rake or hoe diagonally on the bed—teeth or blade facing up—and gently press the wooden handle into the soil so that it makes a uniform depression along its entire length, all the way to the opposite corner. At the chosen spacing (say 3 inches, the spacing distance for spinach), make a series of these depressions on either side of the first, repeating the process until the bed is marked with diagonal drills in one direction.

Now, using the same 3-inch spacing, crisscross the first set of diagonals until the bed looks like the lattice crust of an applie pie.

Place a seed at every point of intersection, firm in place, and cover with soil to the appropriate depth. Firm again gently. Each seed will be exactly 3 inches from its neighbor and you will have the most efficiently planted spinach bed in town.

Lettuce, radicchio, or brassica seedlings, among others, may be transplanted into the garden in the same pattern, although the spacing between plants will be greater than for seeds—usually 10 to 16 inches, depending upon varieties.

The Choice Is Yours

Experimenting in the garden has always been a source of pleasure for me. I like to try new techniques, to compare them with my "tried and true" methods. It's fun. If something doesn't work, I like to be able to figure out why so I don't repeat the same mistakes. For this reason I try my best to keep accurate records.

In the end, we want to be able to pick our own good-tasting vegetables—that's the point, isn't it? Whichever method you choose for growing your salad garden—single rows, wide rows, raised beds, or double-dug beds—as long as you enjoy the activity of gardening and treat your plants with care, you will meet with success.

CARE AND MAINTENANCE OF SALAD CROPS

The principal features of plant care are thinning, watering, mulching, weeding, and controlling pests and diseases. Let's briefly consider them in order.

Thinning

Though I've already mentioned the need for thinning, it bears some further discussion. In an old movie whose title I can no longer recall, a ship has sunk and the survivors are crowded miserably together in a single lifeboat that is too small to carry them all. Water and food are in desperately short supply. The beleaguered captain, determined to act for the greater good, is forced to make life and death decisions: who shall stay and who must go overboard.

The analogy may be somewhat melodramatic, but when you think about it, the same thing must happen in the garden. Seeding by hand—hardly an exact science—makes it next to impossible to avoid sowing more thickly than you had planned to. Vying desperately for limited sustenance, overcrowded plants will soon become sickly and bug-infested, and the entire crop may be ruined. If you hate to pull up little seedlings, however crowded, consider it this way: For every plant you sacrifice you'll be saving several others.

Which seedlings shall stay and which shall go? Choose the plants that look best and are in approximately the right place. Check each listing for optimum spacing between plants, and then, using a pair of sharp scissors, snip off at ground level—*don't uproot*—the ones that

46

The Salad Lover's
GARDEN

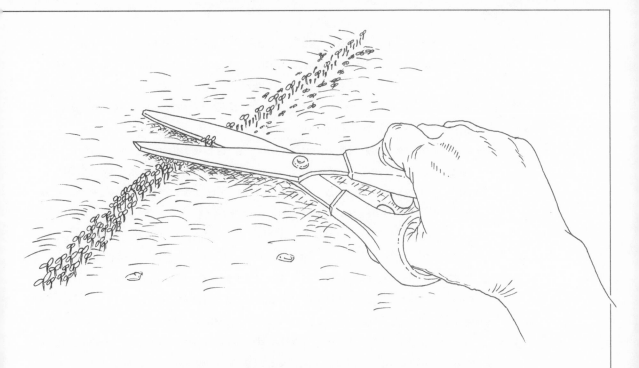

have to go. (If you uproot, you might damage the intertwined roots of plants you want to keep.) There's no need to do all your thinning at once. Make your first thinning soon after the seedlings emerge, and follow up over the next few weeks a little at a time. In fact, with lettuce, carrots, spinach, and a host of other salad gardens, these thinnings can go directly into your salad bowl.

Watering

In gardening, as in all things, there applies the great law of limiting factors. Simply stated, the law dictates that a plant will only be as productive as the least of its vital growth components. You can give a plant a full 100 percent of its air, light, nutrient, and support requirements; but if you supply only 60 percent of its required moisture, the plant will only produce to 60 percent of its inherent capacity.

How much water does a plant need? In order to fulfill its job description as a general life source and medium in which nutrients are dissolved and passed along to plant roots, water must be supplied at a steady, moderate rate over the course of the growing season.

The words "steady" and "moderate" again are hardly precise, and some authorities translate them quantitatively to read "1 inch of water per week." But even that is an arcane standard unless you've got sophisticated equipment to measure the rainfall and then determine how much you need to add, if any, during that week.

The best way to know if your plants are getting enough moisture is to grab a handful of soil and squeeze it. If it's moist, good; if it's dry, now is the time to water. *Never, never wait until plants droop before watering them.* They may never quite recover.

Get to know your garden soil. Feel it after a rain. Does it hold moisture or is it so sandy that moisture drains right through it? Remember, the sandier the soil, the more often you may have to water. Good loam with a high humus content, on the other hand, will hold water like a sponge. As for problem clay soils, adding healthy amounts of humus will allow water to drain through to the root zones of growing plants. And mulching (see page 50) will help reduce surface evaporation.

Watering Techniques

Whenever you water, water deeply. Provide enough water to soak several inches into the soil and the roots will dive deep for it; water shallowly, and plants will develop puny root systems that will, in turn, produce unremarkable plants. The best time of day to water plants is in the cool hours of early morning. Try to avoid evening waterings, because the cool and moist conditions overnight are known to foster the spread of plant disease organisms. If you must water in the evening, do it early enough that plant foliage will dry off before nightfall.

The very best watering system, one that is becoming more popular and affordable, is known as drip irrigation. Briefly explained, the system consists of porous soaker hoses or hoses with tiny trickle holes used in conjunction with various connectors. The hose is laid throughout the garden, either buried in walkways or placed on top of the soil in the middle of planting beds. The hose is then attached to a water

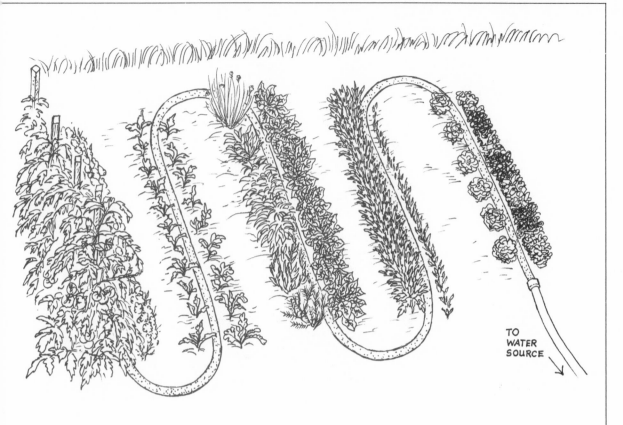

TO
WATER
SOURCE

source and turned on. Water oozes slowly from the pores or holes in the hose, soaking deep into the soil.

You can add automatic timers and minicomputers preset to release the specific quantities of water necessary for your crops. You can even run soluble fertilizers through these systems, which allows you to feed plants while you are watering them.

Drip irrigation is a wonderful way to water small salad gardens which require no more than a couple of hundred feet of hose and a minimum of accessories. The Gardener's Supply catalog is an excellent source (see Appendix).

Overhead sprinklers that rotate or wave from side to side provide a semiautomatic watering system. To automate sprinklers, you set them at various points around the garden when it needs watering and, if you have enough of them, the watering will be accomplished without your having to move them later to cover telltale dry spots. Many sprinklers also come with in-line fertilizer attachments. The only serious drawback to this type of watering is that so much water is lost through evaporation before it ever reaches plant roots. Overhead sprinklers are just not very efficient.

If you don't want to go automatic, get yourself a good hose and a watering wand with a gentle flow and water your plants one at a time. I actually prefer this method at times, because it brings me in direct contact with every plant in the garden. And as the proverb says, "The eye of the farmer fatteneth the land."

Mulching

Mulching, that multivirtued gardening practice of laying down a protective cover on top of the soil, accomplishes several valuable things. It conserves moisture, smothers weeds, moderates soil temperature, and, as it decomposes, bequeaths highly prized humus to the soil. You can mulch your garden with straw, cocoa bean hulls, leaf mold,

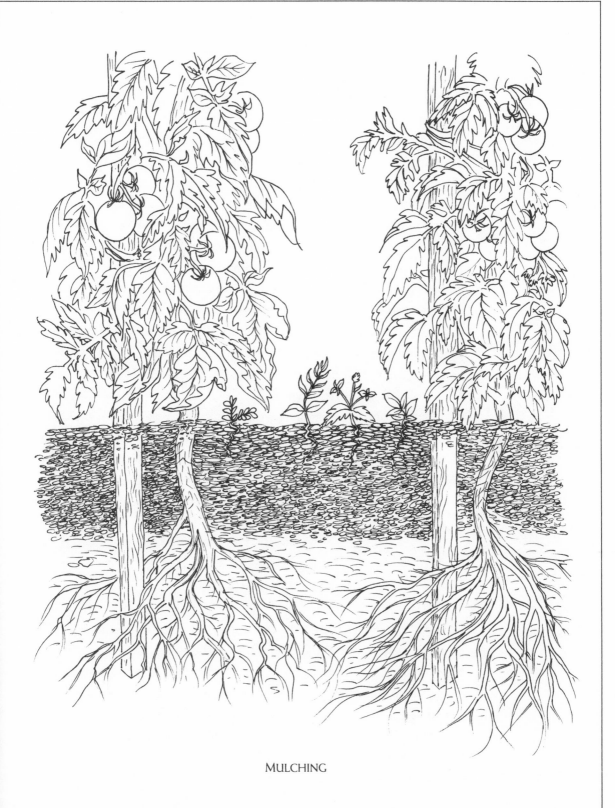

MULCHING

grass clippings, newspaper, or any of a number of other materials.

Many gardeners mulch every part of the garden—walkways and planting beds alike. Studies show that weeds growing in walkways rob crops of more water and nutrients than weeds growing right alongside them in beds, so I have always concentrated my efforts toward making certain my walkways are well mulched—especially if mulching materials are limited. Besides, in intensively planted beds, the foliage creates a natural shade mulch, which does everything an organic mulch does except directly enrich the soil.

If you'd like to mulch right up to the stem of each growing plant, that's fine, but wait until the soil has warmed up before applying the mulch; otherwise the insulating properties of the mulch will keep the soil too cool for some of the heat-loving crops like tomatoes, peppers, and cucumbers. Some gardeners like to lay down black plastic mulch around these crops as soon as they are planted out. In this way heat is gathered easily and quickly, the plants rocket off to a fast start, and the plastic will keep all but the stoutest weeds down. Make slits in the plastic to allow in water.

If you opt for one of the organic mulches just mentioned, lay down several inches of it if you have it; otherwise, just keep adding as materials become available. Some weeds may grow through, but any that do are easy to pull out, roots and all, even in walkways, because the soil is moist and much less compacted owing to its mulch cover.

Weeding

I have a benevolent attitude toward weeds. Don't get me wrong; I don't let them have their way with me. Rather, I choose not to consider them enemies. For one thing, some of them are food. Young chick-weed, lamb's-quarters, purslane, and wild dandelion leaves actually get tossed into my early spring salads along with the lettuce. When they get older, weeds become food for the compost pile. And, finally, when passion drives me to an otherwise choreless garden, there are the weeds giving me something to do.

Any garden soil is packed with weed seeds; deep cultivation, which happens during tilling, will bring them near the surface where, with the help of a little rain, they sprout like the dickens. Annual broadleaf weeds such as pigweed, ragweed, mustard, and lamb's-quarters are easy to deal with if you start early and remain vigilant throughout the season. Annual grasses like crabgrass and goosegrass and several others require similar attention.

But the real pains in the neck to my way of thinking are the perennial grasses, creeping weeds, and broadleaf weeds like dandelion, chicory, plantain, and thistle. The broadleafs have deep roots which are nearly impossible to pull out totally, and any piece of root that remains in the soil will produce a new plant. The perennial grasses and creepers have knotty, hard-to-pull roots with the same sorcerer's apprentice syndrome: The more you deal with them, the more they seem to multiply.

So you must create détente with weeds. Live with those you have, and make certain you don't let the population increase. This you will accomplish by never letting weeds go to seed in the garden— a single mature weed can produce tens of thousands of viable seeds! Two other principal sources of weed seeds which you must forbid entry to are seedy mulch hay and fresh horse and cow manure. Ideally, you should use only straw or otherwise seedless mulches, and compost all stable manure for at least a year. The exception to the fresh manure rule is in double-dug beds, where manure is placed 12 inches down and the beds are never turned. Even so, with reports about excessive, even toxic, levels of nitrate salts transferred from fresh manure to leaf crops, I'd let the stuff sit awhile before using it.

Controlling Pests and Diseases

I like to think my attitude toward the insect world, like my attitude toward weeds, is somewhat evolved. I don't blast poison sprays at anything that crawls or flies only to inspect later the damage I might have done. Instead, I try to be tolerant of insects, at least up to a point.

It's harder, however, to gain a sense of equanimity regarding insects as easily as one might with weeds. Insects, at least a certain few, can actually do physical harm to the plants you have so tenderly cared for from their inception. Insects will suck and chew and otherwise make holes in your young charges, and even carry disease to them. This behavior will bring out the angry parent in you, I guarantee, and all your loathing; it may even provoke you to sudden radical action.

But don't be radical. Year after year I grow wonderful vegetables and flowers and I've never had to resort to the insecticidal/fungicidal arsenal made so handy by the chemical industry. I've had some losses, and heaven knows I've had many an embarrassing cabbage worm show up in my broccoli (at the table). Each year I try harder to outwit these offenders, and each year I get better at it. Here's some of what I've learned.

The best insurance against insect and disease attack is healthy soil. Healthy soil produces strong plants, and studies have shown that insects tend to prey on weaklings. But when insects do go after strong plants, those plants will be better able to weather the attack and, with a little help from you, remain productive.

Avoid planting the same crops in the same spot year after year. Overwintering insects will hatch out in spring and hungrily search out their traditional host crops. Moving the crops even 10 feet away can have some mitigating effect on the new generation of pests. This practice of crop rotation, when practiced systematically, not only fools insects but keeps soil nutrients in balance (because different crops draw different nutrients).

Be hygienic in your garden. Remove standing plants as soon as they've finished producing, especially at the end of the season. In this way you will have eliminated a safe winter haven for certain harmful insects. Also, keep dead leaves and other plant debris picked up to eliminate hiding places for insects and disease organisms.

Try planting a little out of phase. Insects hatch out pretty regularly every season, and also within seasons. Plant out or sow crops a little earlier or later than usual and maybe you'll throw off the insects' biological clocks as well. Keeping notes on when you see certain insects each season is helpful.

Choose disease-resistant varieties. Seed catalogs are very quick to point out that certain varieties are resistant to disease. If certain soilborne diseases have been a problem in your garden, choose resistant varieties whenever you can.

Trap and handpick larger insects. As an alternative to spraying, take yourself out in the garden and go a-hunting. Carry a can with you, and carefully go up and down the rows looking at your plants. Look high and low, side to side, on tops and undersides of leaves, and where leaves join stems. If insects are there, you'll find them. Toss grubs and caterpillars (often called "worms") into the can and dispose of them later by flushing them down the toilet or squashing them. As for slow fliers like striped cucumber beetles or Mexican bean beetles, you may have no other choice but to snatch 'em and smoosh 'em (gloves come in handy). You don't want to touch slugs (although you may be already convinced that you don't want to touch *any* bug), so lure them into shallow dishes of beer, or lay out boards or large cabbage leaves under which they will crawl for protection from the sun. Turn over the board or leaves, gather up with a trowel the slugs that have been collected, and dump these slimy critters into your can.

Control insects biologically. You'll be delighted to know that some of the insect marauders in your garden are actually prey for other insects, those we like to call the "good" insects. Ladybugs, lacewing flies, braconids, and Trichogramma wasps are individually capable of scarfing down hundreds of insects each day. Problem is, there may not be enough of these predatory insects in your garden. The solution: Order them by the pint or quart from specialty garden supply houses. Ten thousand ladybugs (a pint's worth) will cover 2,000 square feet of garden and may put an end to your aphid problem forever. Gardens Alive! and The Necessary Catalogue are two sources of biological controls (see the Appendix).

Another effective biological control for several injurious soft-bodied garden insects is a lethal bacterium known as *Bacillus thuringiensis* or Bt. Sold under the commercial names Dipel and Thuricide, this

55

safe insect control can be either dusted or sprayed on affected crops. The insects ingest the treated leaves, the bacteria are released into their systems, and it's good-bye, baby. And let me tell you, it works. If you're dusting, do it in the morning when the leaves are still moist with dew, and the dust will adhere better.

Make your own homemade brews. I read many years ago that insects by and large are repelled by anything malodorous—that is, with a sharp, pungent smell. This information launched me on a course of experimentation, the results of which I am afraid to say are hardly what one might call scientific evidence. Nevertheless, I am certainly not alone in the quest for the ultimate home-brewed insect repellent, as will be attested to by the many recipes you are likely to find in modern gardening books with an organic bent. Here are some of my most successful ingredients: garlic, onion, cayenne pepper, white pepper, fish innards, and dishwashing detergent.

Try mixing various proportions in a pint of water, throw into a blender for a minute, strain, and pour into a spray bottle such as one that once held window-cleaning fluid. If the result proves effective, which according to my experience it sometimes will, repeat applications regularly, particularly after a rain.

Another fairly effective, nontoxic brew is lime water. Simply dissolve a cup of garden lime in a quart of water and spray onto the leaves of plants affected by flea beetles (just about any whose leaves are peppered with tiny holes, but most notably mustard, tomatoes, eggplant, and potatoes) and striped cucumber bettles (cucumbers and melons). The spray, when it dries, leaves a whitish cast on the leaves. Reapply as necessary. Also, Safer insecticidal soap works well for me. But if it doesn't get rid of *your* flea beetles, as a last resort you may wish to try rotenone or pyrethrum, insecticides processed from natural sources but extremely toxic.

Common Garden Pests

INSECT PEST	PLANTS AFFECTED	SYMPTOMS	CONTROL
Asparagus Beetle Blue-black with yellow-orange square spots on wing covers, ¼ inch long. Larva is longer, olive/gray with black legs, head. Both adult and larva prey on plants	Asparagus	Foliage eaten and shoots disfigured.	• Cultivate deeply and reduce garden trash (winter habitat of beetle). • Interplant with tomatoes, nasturtiums, calendulas. • Dust with phosphate rock or bone meal.
Aster Leafhopper Green-yellow with six black spots, ⅛ inch long. Nymph is gray.	Lettuce, celery, carrots, and other plants.	Leaves turn brown and die (from aster yellows disease).	• Grow plants in sheltered area. • Cover with netting for protection.
Beet Leafhopper Pale yellow or green, wedge-shaped, ⅛ inch long. Also called whitefly, it is a vector of curly top disease.	Beets, beans, tomatoes, cucumbers, spinach, squash, many flowers.	Plant develops curly top disease, which produces pronounced leaf veins, curled brittle leaves, stunted growth. Plant may die.	• Clean weeds from or around garden. • Remove plants with symptoms.
Cabbage Looper Striped pale green worm, 1½ inches long. Loops or doubles up as it crawls. Eggs are greenish white, on surface of leaves.	All members of the cabbage family, tomatoes, parsley, lettuce, celery, and some flowers.	Leaves eaten, eggs laid on leaves.	• Infect and kill with *Bacillus thuringiensis*.

Common Garden Pests

INSECT PEST	PLANTS AFFECTED	SYMTPOMS	CONTROL
Cabbage Worm White with a tapered end, ⅓ inch wide. Adult fly is small, dark gray.	Cabbage, broccoli, radishes, cauliflower, cress, celery.	Young plants yellow, wilt, and die. Maggots carry bacterial soft rot and blackleg, attacking stem just below soil surface and producing brown tunnels in plant tissue.	• Plant or transplant early to avoid egg-laying flies. • Cover soil next to stem with tar paper to discourage eggs. • Cover rows with cheesecloth or netting.
Carrot Weevil Copper-colored, ⅛ inch long. Larva is small white grub. Adult winters in garden debris, weeds.	Celery, parsley, carrots.	Foliage eaten or pierced with holes.	• Keep garden free of debris. • Destroy grubs by deep cultivation in spring.
Colorado Potato Beetle Yellow with black stripes, ¼ inch long. Larva is dark red grub. Yellow eggs are laid on underside of leaves.	Also tomatoes, peppers.	Leaves eaten.	• Intercrop with garlic, marigolds, beans. • Handpick eggs, adults. • Spray with extract of basil. • Dust with wheat bran. • Select resistant varieties.
Corn Earworm Yellow, green, or brown caterpillar with yellow head, 2 inches long. Also known as tomato fruitworm. Adult is moth with gray-brown wings.	In addition to corn, tomatoes, beans, cabbage, broccoli, lettuce, peppers, squash.	Buds and unfolding leaves of plants are eaten; also holes chewed in fruits.	• Control larvae with garlic and onion sprays. • Dust with *Bacillus thuringiensis*. • Plant marigolds to repel.

Common Garden Pests

INSECT PEST	PLANTS AFFECTED	SYMPTOMS	CONTROL
Cutworms Larvae are plump, soft-bodied, dull-colored. In soil at base of plant. Disturbed, they coil up. Overwinter in cells below ground surface.	Seedlings of most vegetables including cabbage, beans, tomatoes.	Plant stem chewed off near soil surface; or leaves, fruits, or flowers eaten.	• Keep garden free of weeds and grass to destroy places where cutworm moths can lay eggs. • Cultivate around plant base to find and destroy cutworms. • Make paper collar around stems of transplants; bury collar 1 inch in ground. • Scatter crushed eggshells, damp wood ashes, or sharp builder's sand around plants to discourage worms.
Cyclamen Mites Microscopic in size. Also called strawberry crown mite.	Many plants, including peppers and tomatoes.	Infestation of new leaf and blossom tissue causes it to swell and distort. Larvae burrow into crowns of plants, stunting and weakening them.	• Rotate plantings and keep garden area clean. • Rinse plants in warm water.

Common Garden Pests

INSECT PEST	PLANTS AFFECTED	SYMPTOMS	CONTROL
Flea Beetles Of various colors, and very small: 1/16 inch long. Jump when disturbed. Eggs deposited in soil.	Spinach, tomatoes, and other plants.	Adults feed early in season, leaving holes in leaves. Seedlings especially vulnerable.	• Cultivate deeply and keep garden free of weeds. • Flea beetles dislike shade; plant seed thickly, and thin plants after danger of infestation. • Plant with garlic. • Use garlic spray. • Scatter wood ashes.
Harlequin Bug Black with orange-red markings. Flat and small, 3/8 inch long. Bad odor. Small white eggs.	Cabbage, lettuce.	Stems and leaves pierced by bug sucking juices.	• Plant turnips or mustard greens near cabbage patch to trap. • Collect bugs in trap area. • Control weeds. • Spray with soap and nicotine.
Imported Cabbage Worm Inch-long fuzzy caterpillar; adult is white cabbage butterfly. Eggs laid at base of leaves in early spring.	All members of the cabbage family, lettuce, nasturtiums.	Holes eaten in leaves; green droppings.	• Use *Bacillus thuringiensis*. • Plant tansy, rosemary, and other aromatics. • Protect with cheesecloth or netting to prevent moths laying eggs. • Cultivate and clean up to eliminate hiding places.
Japanese Beetle Shiny copper-green, 1/2 inch long. Grub is about an inch long, curled in soil.	Adult feeds on many plants (beans, for example).	Holes chewed in leaves.	• Handpick and destroy beetles. • Plant geraniums to repel.

Common Garden Pests

INSECT PEST	PLANTS AFFECTED	SYMPTOMS	CONTROL
Leafhoppers Variety of small wedge-shaped insects.	Lettuce, celery, beans, tomatoes, cucumbers, spinach.	Plants weakened and stunted; leaves become brittle or yellow. Sap-sucking insects cause variety of diseases.	• Control weeds. • Remove diseased plants. • Use resistant varieties.
Leaf Miners Insect larvae that tunnel between leaf surfaces.	Spinach, beets, peppers, cabbage, and other plants.	Foliage yellows or appears blotched. Tunnel can sometimes be seen on leaf surface.	• Remove and burn infested foliage. • Cultivate and weed well.
Mexican Bean Beetle Copper-colored with round back and black spots. Larva is fuzzy, yellow, covered with spines. Overwinters in garden trash.	Pods, stems, and foliage of many kinds of beans (and other plants).	Foliage eaten.	• Handpick. • Clean up harvest debris. • Plant early to avoid infestation. • Destroy yellow eggs. • Interplant with nasturtiums, garlic. • Spray with mixture of turnips and corn oil.
Nematodes Also called eelworms, a microscopic form of roundworms. Many are parasites of plant tissue, feeding on surface of plants or from within.	Variety of garden plants.	Flowers, leaves, stems, or root structure malformed; dieback or chlorosis of foliage. Openings from feedings invite disease organisms.	• Sterilize soil (have sample analyzed). • Rotate plantings. • Interplant marigolds.

Common Garden Pests

INSECT PEST	PLANTS AFFECTED	SYMPTOMS	CONTROL
Onion Maggot White, legless, ⅓ inch long. Adult fly is ¼ inch long, is brown, and has humped back and wings. Eggs laid along base of plant or in bulbs.	Onions, at all stages of growth.	Feeding by maggot on lower part of stem, or bulb.	• Avoid planting in rows; scatter throughout garden. • Cover with layer of sand or wood ashes. • Red varieties most resistant; yellow more resistant than white.
Parlseyworm Also known as carrot worm and celery worm. Green 2-inch larva has yellow-dotted black band on each segment. When disturbed, emits strong odor and shows two orange horns. Adult is black swallowtail butterfly.	Celery, carrots, dill, parlsey.	Foliage eaten.	• Handpick.
Pickleworm Caterpillar is ¾ inch long, green or copper. Younger worm is yellow with black spots. Adult moth is yellow.	Most cucurbits.	Boring into buds, blossoms, vines, and fruits.	• Plant early to avoid. • Kill hibernating pupae by turning over soil in fall. • Clean up plant refuse after harvesting. • Plant squash as trap crop.
Potato Leafhopper Wedge-shaped and green, with white spots.	Also beans, lettuce.	Causes hopperburn: Tips and sides of leaves curl up, become yellow and brittle. Plant's growth is stunted.	• Cover plants with netting for first month. • Trap with black fluorescent lights.

Common Garden Pests

INSECT PEST	PLANTS AFFECTED	SYMPTOMS	CONTROL
Slugs and Snails Not insects, but can be garden pests. Soft bodies covered by thick mucous membrane; leave silvery trail on leaves or paths.	Garden foliage.	Eaten leaves; slimy trails on leaves.	• Lay boards in the garden for traps. • Handpick. • Sprinkle with salt. • Set out saucers of stale beer which will trap and drown offenders. • Mulch with oak leaves, tobacco stem meal, and wormwood tea.
Spotted or Striped Cucumber Beetle Adult is ¼ inch long, with striped or spotted yellow-green body. Larva is larger, white.	Early beans, cucumbers, asparagus, tomatoes, cabbage, and peas, among other plants.	Some defoliation; spread of several bacterial diseases, such as cucumber wilt.	• Cultivate to destroy larvae. • Plant crops later in season. • Mulch heavily.
Squash Bug Brown-black, 1 inch long or less. Also called stinkbug from bad odor. Nymph has reddish head, legs; green to brown body. Red eggs laid in clusters.	Vine crops, especially squash.	Plant wilts and dies.	• Plant marigolds, radishes, nasturtiums. • Control weeds. • Rotate crops. • Handpick insects and eggs.
Squash Vine Borer Caterpillar, 1 inch long; white with brown head and legs. Adult is moth with clear wings, orange and black body.	Squash and other cucurbits.	Sudden wilting; yellow, sawdustlike deposits at stem base, from tunneling into stem by larva.	• Slit stem and take out larva. • Set plants later to confound insect feeding cycle. • Set plants early so they are established before insect eggs hatch in June.

Common Garden Pests

INSECT PEST	PLANTS AFFECTED	SYMPTOMS	CONTROL
Stalk Borer Striped, 1-to-1½-inch-long caterpillar. Adult moth is gray with white wing spots.	Many plants including peppers, tomatoes.	Stems break, leaves wilt. Small round hole appears in stem where caterpillar enters.	• Handpick • Remove infested stems. • Prevent with good cultivation, weed control.
Tarnished Plant Bug Small adult is green-brown, with black spots. Nymph is similar, smaller.	Beans, beets, cabbage, cucumbers.	Plant wilts and dies from poison injected by feeding bug.	• Dust with sabadilla, an insecticide made from the seed of a South American plant in the lily family.
Thrips Small, barely visible, winged insects.	Many plants, including beans.	Foliage damaged by insects sucking juice; becomes bleached, silvered, withered. Flowers and fruits may be damaged.	• Control weeds. • Mulch with aluminum foil. • Spray with oil and water mixture, or add tobacco.
Tomato Hornworm Green with a horn on its back end; up to 4 inches long. Adult sphinx moth has wingspan of 4 to 5 inches.	Tomatoes, dill, peppers.	Leaves and sometimes fruit eaten by larvae.	• Handpick • Dust with hot pepper.
Vegetable Weevil Adult is buff-colored beetle, with V marking on wing covers. Green or cream-colored larva.	Beets, cabbage, cauliflower, lettuce, onions, tomatoes, and others.	Foliage eaten at night; often whole plant defoliated, starting at crown.	• Rotate crops. • Cultivate to destroy pupae underground. • Keep garden neat.

Plant Diseases

DISEASE	PLANTS AFFECTED	SYMPTOMS	CONTROL
Anthracnose	Beans, cucumbers, squash, eggplant, tomatoes, potatoes.	Reddish brown or black spots on leaves, stems, pods.	• Establish two-year rotation of planting areas. • Don't work in garden when it's wet. • Don't plant peppers near beans. • Pull up and burn affected plants.
Blackleg	Cabbage family.	Lower stem blackens all the way around. Young plants yellow, wilt, die.	• Rotate plantings. • Remove garden debris. • Before planting, soak seed in hot water (122°F) for twenty minutes.
Black rot	Cabbage family.	Blackened veins. Stem shows blackened ring when sliced across. Leaves yellow and drop. Bacteria live in soil and seeds.	• See Blackleg.
Blight	Tomatoes.	Small, irregular, dark brown spots, sometimes with target markings. Sunscald and leathery spots near stem.	• Rotate plantings. • Remove residue after harvest.
Blossom-end rot	Tomatoes, peppers.	Dark sunken spots on blossom end of fruits.	• Keep water supply constant, especially during dry weather. • Add lime. • For eating, cut away affected part.

Plant Diseases

DISEASE	PLANTS AFFECTED	SYMPTOMS	CONTROL
Clubroot	Cabbage family.	Roots become enlarged and "clubbed," and crack or rot. Affected plants may wilt during day but recover at night. Young plants usually die; yields reduced on established plants.	• Establish a four-year rotation. • Add lime to soil to discourage acid-loving organisms.
Damping-off	Beans, lettuce, peas, tomatoes.	Seedlings won't emerge, or if they do, they often wilt and topple over. Stems show constriction just below soil line.	• For starting seeds indoors, use sterile soil mixes. • Don't crowd or overwater plants.
Leaf spot	Beets, chard.	Leaves have small tan spots with purple borders. Leaves may drop later.	• See Anthracnose.
Mildew, downy	Cucumbers, some greens.	Yellowish or brownish spots on older leaves. Leaves dry, curl, and die. Fruits not affected. Disease spread by windborne spores.	• Keep plants thinned for good air circulation. • Remove diseased foliage, burn. • Spray home brew mixture of two ounces horsetail herb in one gallon water; repeat often. • Remove all crop residues.
Mildew, powdery	Cucurbits, beans.	Powdery white growth on stems, leaves. Leaves turn yellow or brown.	• See Mildew, downy.

Plant Diseases

DISEASE	PLANTS AFFECTED	SYMPTOMS	CONTROL
Mosaic	Beans, tomatoes, celery, peppers, cucurbits.	Leaves are mottled and curled, become yellow, and die. Cucumbers become misshapen and warty. Bean and tomato plants become stunted.	• Grow resistant varieties. • Control disease-carrying aphids. • Keep tall weeds or grass trimmed around garden. • Smokers should not handle tomato or pepper plants, because this may transmit disease. • Remove and burn affected plants immediately.
Pink root	Onions, shallots.	Roots turn pink, shrivel, die. Newly formed roots also become infected, reducing overall bulb size.	• Plant resistant varieties.
Rust	Asparagus, beans.	Small reddish or dark brown powdery blisters on all plant parts. Plants usually don't survive.	• Plant resistant varieties. • Remove and burn affected plant parts; wash clippers before using on other plants. • Avoid working around plants when wet.
Wilt, bacterial	Cucurbits.	Runners wilt, plant shrivels. Disease organism lives in intestinal tract of cucumber beetle. Young plants most susceptible.	• Control cucumber beetle. • Protect new plants with hot caps or other covers to keep beetles from landing, but don't overheat.

Plant Diseases

DISEASE	PLANTS AFFECTED	SYMPTOMS	CONTROL
Wilt, fusarium and verticillium	Tomatoes, peas.	Yellowing and wilting of foliage, beginning with lower leaves. Stems turn brown and die. Tomatoes on affected plants will be sunburned as foliage drops.	• Plant resistant varieties. • Establish three-year rotation. • Don't save seed from affected plants.
Yellows	Cabbage, lettuce, spinach, celery.	Foliage yellows, plants become stunted, rarely forming heads. Disease spread by leafhoppers.	• Control leafhoppers.

4

Special Salad Growing Routines

I said earlier that true salad lovers are hardly content with a run-of-the-mill plate of lettuce. We look for flavor, color, tenderness, texture, and variety—especially variety, that surprise ingredient! This is particularly the case halfway through the season, when we've prepared and eaten 150 salads, and we're starting to get a little bored. Even dedicated salad lovers sometimes need a lift, something new and exciting.

This chapter is devoted to those special strategies aimed at keeping new salad ingredients coming from the garden all the time.

The subject of starting garden plants indoors is almost always introduced in the context of "getting a jump on the growing season." But starting seeds indoors is also, and quite logically (as you will see), the key to the successful succession cropping of leafy salad vegetables. Here's why.

It is generally in late spring or early summer when your first leaf crops mature in the garden and you make your final harvest of them. The weather has warmed up quite a bit by then, and soil temperatures are up in the 80°F range. Lettuce, spinach, and chicory seed will germinate miserably or not at all in soil much warmer than 70°F. For keeping a fresh batch of seedlings of all kinds ready to fill vacancies in the garden, you have a couple of choices. You can keep a nursery bed or open cold frame partially shaded and perpetually moist so the soil neither overheats nor crusts over. Or you can start plants indoors where temperature and moisture are easily and reliably controlled all season long.

If you've never started your own plants from seed, this is going to be great fun for you. It gives the gardening experience a meaningful totality, for you will have had your hand in every phase of the growing process.

One word of caution, however. Seedlings grown indoors require considerable care: regular feeding and watering, a steady source of light, and adequate ventilation. Droopy seedlings recovering from an imposed drought may never be the productive plants you'd intended them to be once they reach the garden. So launch this phase of your salad gardening adventure only if you have the time, the means, and the will to bring it off.

Having decided, I hope, to forge bravely ahead, you will need to arm yourself with some basic materials. Most important to start with are a table and some work space. A hollow-core door resting on a pair of sawhorses makes an ideal planting table for a seasonal setup, though more permanent installations can be bought or built. Put the table someplace you and your plants can call your own for six months without the family screaming bloody murder.

Planting Containers

Anything that can hold an inch or two of potting soil is technically a fit container for starting seeds. I've used hand-built seeding flats, egg cartons, polystyrene foam cups (before I knew they were harmful to the earth's delicate ozone layer), and even aluminum roasting pans (okay as long as you don't try to move them; when you do, the soil shifts and seedlings tumble). I've also used an ever changing assortment of wonderful products, from individual peat pellets and peat pots to seeding flats of all kinds, including germination chambers that have automatic waterers and are covered by clear plastic domes like miniature greenhouses. Most garden seed and supply catalogs will offer you a whole range of choices.

Potting Mix

The very best medium for starting seeds is a sterilized mix of peat moss and vermiculite, which is available at all garden stores under various names. I've used Pro-Mix with excellent results for years. Standard potting soil and compost are far too rich to use as media for starting seeds. Young seedlings planted in them grow too quickly, becoming leggy and ending up in the garbage heap not long afterward.

It is possible in many garden supply catalogs to find a useful device called a soil block maker. You fill its small cubicles with a specially prepared planting mix, then press down upon a plunger, and out come perfect cubes of compressed planting medium, just right for planting individual seeds. As the seedlings grow, their roots spread to the outer limits of the cube and become "air-pruned"—that is, their roots are discouraged from stretching into open air and so curl back into the cube, creating plants with vigorous, compact root systems just waiting to be planted out.

Nothing could be simpler than sowing seeds in individual blocks or plastic cells. Make the soil blocks as just described and place them in a tray that has drainage holes. Fill plastic cells to within ½ inch of the top with premoistened planting mix; then smooth the surface with your fingers and place the cells in trays.

Press two seeds gently onto the soil surface, making sure there is good seed-to-soil contact. Next, using a food strainer, sift a dusting of planting mix over the seeds and gently firm the surface. Finally, moisten the surface with a plant mister.

Sowing seeds in flats requires a bit more patience, but the principles and many of the procedures are entirely the same as for soil blocks and plastic cells. First, fill the seed flat with premoistened planting mix to within ½ inch of the top, and level off the surface with a flat board. Make sure that all the corners are filled and that there are no gaping holes in the surface into which small seeds could slide and slip beneath their optimum germination depth. The object of sowing in seed flats is to start a fairly large number of plants at the same time (a standard flat might easily hold as many as fifty seedlings) without dangerously overcrowding them.

The first step in planting a flat is to make shallow rows or "drills" in the surface of the medium. Gently press a common ¼-inch dowel (or even a pencil if you have no dowel) into the soil across the short dimension of the flat. Use just enough pressure to create an indentation of no more than ⅛ inch. Try to keep seeds at least ½ inch apart.

Spacing is no problem with tomato and pepper seeds, which are relatively large and easy to control. Lettuce seed, on the other hand— as well as seeds of chicory, onions, the cabbages, and other greens— are tiny and virtually weightless, making overseeding a distinct possibility. You pinch up a few seeds in the hope of being able to drop one at a time over a designated site, but you hardly go an inch or two along your designated row and find that you have already spilled eight seeds in one little spot, left the next inch a total blank, and dropped four seeds in the next spot. You try to pick up some of the excess, but they blend in with the soil and you haven't got a ghost of a chance. The only way to do it right is with a tool. It's a tedious process, but for years I've had good luck with pointed tweezers. I lose a few seeds every now and again, but then, so what?

Pour a little mound of seeds into the palm of one hand; peck out one seed at a time with the tweezers and lay it in place on top of the soil mix. The English horticulturalist Joy Larkcom claims that a seed, first placed onto the moistened tip of a shard of window glass, will drop in place as soon as it touches the soil. I've never tried it; if you do, exercise the proper caution.

However you do it, once the seeds are actually in place, cover them with a sifting of planting mix, firm the surface gently with a board, and spray with a mister until the surface glistens.

Be Sure to Label Everything Carefully

As soon as the seeds are planted, label each container carefully with an indelible marker so you will remember what's what. Distinguishing between lettuce and tomatoes once the seedlings emerge is not the issue. Rather, you'll want to keep your Lolla Rosa lettuce seedlings separated from your Sangria lettuce seedlings, and your Marmande tomatoes from your Sweet 100, because all those little guys of the same species tend to look alike when they're young.

Once everything is labeled, place each tray into a plastic bag and shut it tight with a wire tie to preserve moisture during the germination process. This practice, however, robs the interior of the germination chamber of air, which could permit the formation of fungus organisms and even result in plant disease. It is therefore essential that the bags be opened every day for an hour or so to allow for a little ventilation.

Place the covered trays in a warm spot where temperatures are above 70°F—on top of the refrigerator is a good place—until germination occurs. Then remove the plastic bags and get your young seedlings under light.

Container mates, whether they're planted in soil blocks, plastic cells, or especially flats, should have the same estimated time of germination. Keep all your tomatoes together in the same trays, your cabbage together, your lettuces together, so the seeds in each tray germinate roughly simultaneously. If some plants germinate in a seed flat and others don't because they are of another species, you'll have to immediately prick out the seedlings which have sprouted, put them in their own containers, and return the remainder to darkness to germinate. This is a cumbersome and entirely avoidable dilemma. Whatever you do, do *not* leave newly germinated plants in darkness while hoping that the rest will soon pop up, or you'll end up with a gnarly mass of leggy louts who will never be able to stand on their own. So remember what I say: Seeds that stay together should reach the light of day together.

Light

As soon as your seedlings have germinated, get them under light. The most convenient system for my money is having all your plants in their trays on the aforementioned worktable bathing in the green/ white/blue blaze of fluorescent tubes suspended only inches above their young crowns. Get yourself an inexpensive electric timer, plug it into the wall socket, plug the lights into it, and set the device to give twelve to sixteen hours of light each day. Keep the room cool— between 60° and 65°F.

If you can't set up lights, you can set up small tables at sunny windows, or even set very small plant trays directly on windowsills. You'll notice your plants will start to lean in the direction of the light source. When this happens, turn the trays around until they start leaning again and just continue the process. Move the plants at least several feet from the windows during winter nights, as the temperatures right next to the glass fluctuate wildly, especially if there are drafts. Conversely, July's midday sun may be too strong at the window for young seedlings; they'll perform better in indirect light.

Transplanting

No matter how carefully you may have seeded your flat, plants will start to crowd themselves when they've grown their first set of true leaves. Removing them from the seed flat to another container is a simple yet enjoyable phase of indoor gardening. Transplant into another flat (only this time plants are spaced 2 to 3 inches apart), individual cells in four-packs or six-packs, or individual 2- or 3-inch pots.

To accomplish the task, you will need either a small dibble stick, a butter knife, or even an old spoon—anything that will reach under a seedling's roots and dislodge the young plant. Make sure the containers to which the plants are to be moved are filled with moist planting mix which has been moderately fertilized. For this you can use bagged dehydrated manure, a bit of your own compost, or liquid fish emulsion in the prescribed dilution. I actually prefer the fish emulsion in spite of its aroma, as it takes up no storage room to speak of.

First, water well the plants about to be moved. Using the dibble or knife as a lever, gently lift out a seedling, being sure to hold it *by its leaves*. Under no circumstances should you hold the plant by its delicate stem, for once that tender conduit of water and nutrients between root and leaf is damaged, the seedling is a goner and is best sent off to the compost heap. On the other hand, if, during the transplanting process, a leaf were to be accidentally snapped off or torn, another would grow soon enough.

While holding the seedling in one hand, with your free hand holding the dibble, poke a small hole in the soil of the container-in-waiting. The hole should be just large enough to accommodate the seedling's young root-threads. Gently deposit the plant into the hole. At the proper depth, the soil will barely touch the plant's lower leaves. Use your fingers to firm the soil gently around the stem of the plant, driving out air pockets which at this critical time might tend to dry out the delicate roots. Space the plants 2 inches apart, and place them

*Special Salad
Growing Routines*

under lights or in indirect sunlight. Wait a few days before letting the sun shine directly on them, even in winter.

Lettuce, endive, onions, and other hardy salad plants can stay in these new quarters until it's time to plant them outdoors. But your peppers and tomatoes, which need more time indoors, should go from seed flat to 3-inch pots when they have their first true leaves, and from there to even larger pots or containers when they are about 6 inches tall. Here they will remain until they are ready for hardening off.

Hardening Off

Hardening off is the process by which seedlings grown under cover are introduced gradually to the harsher conditions of outdoor living: hotter and colder temperatures, wind, rain, drought, unrelenting sun. The process is generally begun a week or so before plants will be set out in the garden proper, where they must survive more or less on their own (I say more or less because we gardeners are a nurturing lot and finds ways to protect our own).

Start by reducing frequency of waterings and allowing in outside air through an open window for up to a week. Move plants away from the window at night to protect against cold blasts. Then move the plants outdoors to a spot sheltered from direct sun or wind, but bring them indoors at night. Repeat the process for three or four days, and then begin leaving them outside around the clock. This will cause you some minor anxiety, but never fear, these plants are going to survive. Of course, if some unexpected, wayward frost is predicted for their first nights out, by all means either cover the plants or bring them inside.

If you have a cold frame, you have an ideal environment for hardening off young plants that began life indoors in winter. (Later in the season you can start new seedlings right in the cold frame.) Once the plants have had their few protected days outdoors, they can be placed inside the cold frame. When the temperature outdoors is cold, keep the glass cover in place; when it is warmer, raise the glass several inches or more depending on the temperature. Keep a thermometer handy inside the cold frame so you can see when the temperature rises.

Planting Out

No matter how carefully you hardened off your plants, removing them from their containers in order to set them into garden soil is going to expose those roots to air and light, and is going to unsettle them. Even plants grown in soil blocks are not immune from mild shock. That said, let me assure you there is nothing to fear as far as the safety and future productivity of these plants are concerned if you follow a few simple guidelines.

In order to minimize transplant shock, do your transplanting on a cloudy day when there is little wind. If you've taken a day off from work to do the transplanting and it happens to be sunny, that will be okay if you wait until late in the day. If it's very blustery in addition, think twice about doing the planting. Why risk all your hard work? Better wait until the weekend.

Water the beds where your young plants will be spending their time, and dig your planting holes in advance, adding a handful of compost or aged manure in the bottom of each hole for good measure. Set each plant into its own hole, generally about an inch deeper than it stood in its previous container. Fill in the hole with soil and then firm the plant into place, driving out any lingering air pockets.

For the next two weeks, keep these plants well watered. And to protect them against damage from frost, wind, or sun, place a hot cap, cloch, jelly jar, or plastic milk jug with the bottom cut off right over each plant. These days, every garden catalog offers some sort of spun polyester sheeting that can be thrown over an entire row to protect plants. The material is so lightweight that it is actually pushed upward as the plants grow. For crops especially vulnerable to early insect attack, such as cucumbers (striped cucumber beetle), the cabbage family, tomatoes, and eggplant (white cabbage butterfly and flea beetle), this material—known sometimes as Reemay—is a godsend.

SEEDLING CROPS

When we think of lettuce, most of us conjure a mature head—the sort we're likely to find in the produce section of the supermarket. But lettuce and many other vegetables and herbs can be harvested at various stages of their growth cycle to provide enormous variety in the salad bowl.

When cut extremely young—at the seedling stage—leaves are remarkably tender and delicious. Amazingly, if the plants are left in the ground, they will grow again, actually yielding several harvests, a habit which has earned them the title of "cut-and-come-again" crops. You may choose to cut the second growth also at the seedling stage, wait until the leaves are somewhat more developed, or even wait until some have reached full maturity. As you see, a single sowing can make mighty efficient use of limited space.

The fastest way to sow a seedling crop is to broadcast the seeds, more or less willy-nilly, over a prepared seedbed. Severely overcrowded seedlings can suffer from all sorts of maladies, so try your best not to overseed. That, however, is easier said than done, so be prepared to do some early thinning (seedlings should stand about ½ inch apart). Firm the seeds in place with the flat blade of a hoe, a board, or your hands, and cover with light soil. If your soil runs toward clay, cover the seeds with screened compost or even your peat-based indoor planting mix instead of soil. This will ensure easy emergence for the seedlings. Don't let the seedbed dry out during germination; thereafter, make sure the young plants receive adequate moisture.

Seedling crops can be cut anytime after they have grown their first set of true leaves. But whether you cut them two to three weeks after sowing, or wait until the leaves have reached midgrowth (five to six weeks), the harvesting process is the same.

Your tool of choice is a very sharp knife, though a pair of scissors is also good for making small snippets. Holding the tops of the leaves with one hand, cut away a few handfuls with the knife, as much as you need for a salad, leaving a good inch of stem standing.

In the following days, just keep working your way down the row, cutting as much as you need. By the time you've reached the far end of the row, the first patch you cut will be ready to cut again. After two or more cuttings, the leaves will start to lose their sweet taste and tender texture, and that is the time to uproot whatever remains and plant the bed with another crop. "Get 'em in and get 'em out so you can try something new" must be the salad gardener's motto.

Look for more information on seedling and cut-and-come-again crops under individual vegetables and herbs in Chapter 5.

BLANCHING

One of the more interesting techniques the salad gardener must master is the practice of blanching. Blanching, or making things white, is accomplished (oddly enough) by imposing darkness on the plant. You can either bring darkness to the plant or bring the plant to darkness. The first happens in the garden, the second in your basement or a cool closet.

Blanching sweetens and tenderizes leaves as it whitens them. Normally bitter chicories develop creamy-colored and mild-flavored leaves when they are blanched. The frequently tough outer leaves of romaine lettuce remain soft when plants are blanched as they approach maturity.

There are several ways to blanch plants. You can tie the leaves together with string, as is traditionally done with cauliflower, to keep its curds milky white. Some plants, such as curly endive and dandelion, can be covered with pots, boxes, bins, black plastic cloches, and even soil to exclude light. Chicory (radicchio) is usually blanched by transplanting to a darkened area, such as a covered cold frame, under benches in a greenhouse, or an indoor location such as a basement, closet, or attic.

Yet another technique, known as "forcing," calls for digging roots or entire plants, bringing them indoors, and actually forcing them to grow leaves in the darkness. During the process, they become blanched.

We will discuss blanching techniques for individual vegetables in more detail in the next chapters.

5

Salad Greens
and Herbs

From a simple plate of lettuce leaves or hearts dressed with lemon and oil or a flavorful vinaigrette to a savory dish of mixed greens and garnishes (lettuces, chicory, purslane, arugula, and nasturtium, for example) with a more ambitious dressing with cheese and nuts, leafy greens are the essential ingredients of any salad.

This chapter covers *major* greens (lettuces, chicories, endive, escarole, and spinach), *minor* greens (those generally less central to the salad bowl, but which do wonders for adding an array of interesting flavors—arugula, celtuce, chard, cresses, dandelion, mâche, mustard, and shungiku), and herbs. Cabbages are covered in Chapter 6.

For want of space, not all salad greens and herbs are treated here or elsewhere in this book. But I have provided lists of these here and

there, and you can order additional salad crops from the catalogs listed in the Appendix.

LETTUCE

Lettuce is the jewel of the salad garden because it is the very heart of the salad bowl itself. Young lettuce plants in a variety of pleasing shapes and colors—some green, others tinged with red, still others nearly a full crimson—grow willingly, *eagerly* even, to maturity.

Lettuce has an interesting past. It was worshiped as a phallic symbol by ancient Egyptians. (This may have been romaine, with its upright, narrow heads; romaine was, much later, said to have been introduced to France from Italy by none other than Rabelais himself.) Later on, lettuce was regarded as a symbol of female sexuality around the Mediterranean area as late as the sixteenth century. To compound the confusion, lettuce had also been dubbed *eunuch* by ancient Greeks and recommended to young ascetics as an effective means of controlling sexual passion. It was apparently successful as a remedy, for it was referred to as *astutis*—meaning "incapable of erection"—by women of the time. In fact, in the Greek comedy *The Impotents* (*Astutoi*) by Euboulos, a male character warns his wife that she has only herself to blame if she serves him lettuce for supper.

Modern gardeners classify lettuce along more botanical lines, into four main groups. Of each of these four there are dozens of varieties available, with the number growing each year. Imports from Italy and France have become extremely popular in just the last couple of years: The Cook's Garden catalog, for instance, features more than fifty excellent varieties; Shepherd's Garden Seeds, Johnny's Selected Seeds, and Seeds Blum offer about twenty-five each. I urge you to try as many lettuces as you can fit in your garden from spring through late fall.

1. **Leaf lettuces (also known as loose leaf, salad bowl, or cutting lettuce):** This group forms loose rosettes rather than heads, and all varieties will resprout energetically when cut down young. By and large the texture of loose leaf lettuces is crisp. The colors vary from pale and

LEAF LETTUCE

71

*Salad Greens
and Herbs*

dark green to deep crimson and bronze, with many varieties now showing combinations of color: pale green interiors with red-tinged leaves; green and bronze; pink and crimson. The flavor ranges from almost bland to a stronger, almost woodsy taste. And leaf shape can be deeply curled, savoyed, or quite smooth.

2. **Crisphead:** Often associated with iceberg, this type offers many interesting varieties—all with that crisp, clean flavor which is the trademark of crisphead lettuces. They all form tight heads of green, red, or red and green leaves.

3. **Butterhead:** While the popular Bibb and Boston are familiar varieties, you'll discover many more now available. Neither loose leaf nor crisphead butterheads, one could say, are loose heads of deeply folded leaves with a sweet, buttery flavor. Some varieties are all green; others have green leaves tinged with red or bronze.

4. **Romaine or cos:** This variety features long, upright ribbed leaves with smooth or savoyed tips. Romaine is generally green, but deep red to almost purple-leaved romaines are now available from several seed houses. Plants are generally 8 to 12 inches tall and weigh up to a pound or more at maturity. The tops of the leaves are quite tender and nutty/buttery in flavor, while lower down the leaves are crispy and juicy.

So-called "baby" lettuces, miniatures versions of the crisphead, butterhead, and cos types, are now available in many seed catalogs. See page 79 for varieties.

How to Grow Lettuce

With rich soil and plenty of moisture, you should have little problem raising good lettuce. For spring leaf lettuce, sow seeds directly in the garden as soon as you can work the soil. Make uniform seed drills ¼ to ½ inch deep by laying down your rake or hoe on top of the prepared seedbed, teeth or blade facing up, and pressing lightly on the long handle. Sprinkle seeds as evenly as possible in the drills, and when you're done, cover the seeds with sifted compost or peat moss to prevent the surface from caking over. Firm gently with your hand or the blade of your hoe. Water gently after planting.

A Continuous
Supply of Lettuce

As a salad lover, you will want to aim to have a steady supply of lettuce from as early in the spring to as late in the fall as possible. You can avoid the unfortunate but common feast-or-famine syndrome, wherein you are first inundated by too much lettuce and then frustrated by too little, with a little planning.

Effective succession planning depends upon knowing when a crop goes in and when it is scheduled to mature. Leaf lettuces generally mature within forty-five to sixty days; some varieties, however, keep well beyond their official maturity date because you can maintain them in good condition during hot weather. If you prefer leaf or cutting lettuces young, sow your favorite varieties as frequently as every ten to fourteen days throughout the season—starting plants indoors when the weather becomes too hot outside for decent germination. Otherwise, three sowings of leaf lettuce, about a month apart, will do nicely for the season. And for a seeding mix that bores neither eye nor palate, swirl together in a dish a few pinches of many varieties and sow in the same bed.

Butterheads mature within sixty to seventy-five days, crispheads and romaine from seventy-five to eighty-five days. For an ongoing supply, make sure you've always got some seedlings started somewhere, and plug them into available spaces throughout the season. For succession cropping in hot weather, use new varieties of crisphead, butterhead, and romaine lettuces which have been bred to perform well even in the extreme heat of midsummer.

When starting seeds for succession crops (the weather is likely to be quite warm already), have your cold frame or nursery bed in light shade, or be prepared to keep the seedbed constantly moist and partially shaded with Reemay, cheesecloth, or even a bed sheet. Lettuce seed simply will not germinate in soil warmer than 75°F. Your best bet is probably to start the seeds indoors.

Or, if you prefer, you can broadcast your lettuce. Prepare the seedbed to a smooth finish and then gently sprinkle seed over the soil surface. Working at a height of about a foot is fine, except if it's windy. Then you should place your body between the wind and the seedbed and work even closer to the soil. Firm the seed in place with your hand, the back of a hoe, or a board, cover with a sprinkling of sifted compost or peat moss, and firm again.

Planting head lettuce, especially if you have your heart set on an early crop, is best accomplished by setting transplants as soon as

*Salad Greens
and Herbs*

the soil can be worked. Remember to do your transplanting in the early evening or on a cloudy, windless day (or as close to these unstressful conditions as possible) and follow these simple rules. (1) Prepare planting holes in advance, 8 to 14 inches apart (depending on variety). Into each toss a trowel of compost or aged manure, a dusting of lime or sifted wood ashes and bone meal. Mix together. (2) Give the seedlings a good watering before removing them from the cold-frame bed or the containers in which they are growing. (3) Remove the plants one at a time, strip off a few of the outer leaves, and set each in its own hole at the same depth it was growing previously. Firm the soil around the stem and then water well. Don't let plants dry out and you'll be repaid with a sweet crop. For midsummer succession crops, provide new transplants with shade.

How to Care for Lettuce

Directly seeded lettuces, whether planted in drills or by the broadcast method, will almost certainly require thinning. If you consider the thinnings your first harvest, you will approach the task more willingly. Lettuce thinnings, at any stage, are wonderful to eat. Make your first pass when the seedlings have grown their first set of true leaves; follow with another thinning ten to fourteen days later, when the lettuce plants are a couple of inches tall, and repeat thinnings until the plants are spaced 8 to 14 inches apart, depending on variety. If your succession plan is timed right, you will have other beds to start thinning soon enough.

If your soil is rich enough to begin with, sidedressing the lettuce crop may not be necessary. On the other hand, sprinkling a half-inch layer of compost or old manure on the bed as plants start to make rapid growth, or watering weekly with compost or manure tea, never hurts.

Slugs can be a problem in lettuce beds, particularly when the beds are mulched. If slugs are showing up in larger than normal numbers (some gardeners would say a single slug fits that description),

Broccoli, North Sea Farms, Southampton, N.Y.

Cabbage, North Sea Farms, Southampton, N.Y.

Entrance, Cook's Garden, Londonderry, Vt.

Sam Bittman's garden, Cheshire, Mass.

Basil, Cook's Garden, Londonderry, Vt.

Sam Bittman's garden, Cheshire, Mass.

Chives, Berkshire Garden Center, Stockbridge, Mass.

Radish, North Sea Farms, Southampton, N.Y.

Carrots, North Sea Farms, Southampton, N.Y.

Tomatoes (Laketa),
Cook's Garden, Londonderry, Vt.

Curly endive, Cook's Garden, Londonderry, Vt.

Radicchio (Medusa), Cook's Garden, Londonderry, Vt.

Mei Quing Choy, Cook's Garden, Londonderry, Vt.

Cutting Mix #730, Cook's Garden, Londonderry, Vt.

Tomatoes, Cook's Garden, Londonderry, Vt.

Flowering kale, edible flower garden, Meadowsweet Herb Farm, Shrewsbury, Vt.

remove the mulch. Also, set out boards alongside the beds; the slugs will congregate under the boards to escape the sun's heat. Flip over the boards, scrape off the slugs into a dish, and feed them to your chickens. If you don't have chickens, dump the slimy critters in the trash or otherwise destroy them. Dishes of stale beer or yeast and water will also attract slugs to a watery grave. Be vigilant with slugs or they will mutilate your lettuce.

How to Harvest Lettuce

You can grow leaf lettuce as a seedling crop (see page 66), pick individual leaves as soon as they are big enough to use, or harvest fully mature plants. *How* you harvest salad bowl lettuce determines its longevity and productivity irrespective of *when* you harvest it. If you shear it to within an inch and a half of the soil, the plant will regrow— hence its designation as a "cut-and-come-again" crop. But if you pull it up root and all, the plant can't grow back. If you want to continue harvesting, make sure you leave the roots intact.

Butterhead lettuce matures a week or so after most leaf lettuce. Harvest heads by cutting them off at ground level. Then pull up the roots, mash them with a shovel, and toss them into the compost bin. Romaine heads mature sometime later and can be blanched for a week or two beforehand to sweeten and tenderize the outer leaves. Use milk cartons with tops and bottoms removed, as you would for celery (see page 168). The hearts of romaine are naturally blanched, and the creamy-sweet leaves are magnificent.

Crisphead lettuces mature around the same time as romaine. Feel for good tight heads and harvest as you would other head lettuces. Don't discard the green outer leaves as they do in supermarkets; they are excellent for eating and contain most of the plant's vitamins and minerals.

Recommended Varieties of Lettuce

Romaine or Cos Lettuce

Plants have long leaves, broad at the top, and thick, juicy hearts.

- *Ballon:* Large and pale with fine texture; heat-tolerant. Plant in spring, and again in midsummer for fall harvest.

- *Cosmo:* Spring and fall crops only. Combines crispness of iceberg lettuce with shape and sweetness of romaine. Plants have bright green, savoyed leaves and produce delicious blanched hearts. Susceptible to tipburn in midsummer.

- *Floricos:* Late-maturing, long-standing, with open, unfolded heads. Resists tipburn.

- *Jericho:* Israeli. Sweet and crispy even in hot weather; produces heavy heads. Spring, summer, and fall crops.

- *Parris Island Cos:* Heavier, taller, and earlier than most romaines. Has slightly savoyed leaves and produces creamy white blanched hearts. Grow throughout season; slow to bolt.

- *Red Leprechaun:* Primarily for summer cropping. Savoyed red romaine has succulent, puckered leaves from 8-to-12-inch-tall heads. Mature heads weigh up to a pound; harvest at ¾ pound. Blanched hearts are pale pink on cream.

- *Romance:* French. Smoother, more tender leaves than standard romaine; resistant to mosaic virus and mildew. Very early. Plant in spring and again in midsummer.

- *Rosalita:* Spring and fall crops; winter production in frost-free areas. Medium-size, upright head with purple-red highlights; heart blanches to yellow. Earlier than other red romaines.

- *Rouge D'Hiver:* French heirloom. Large-leaved red romaine, resistant to both heat and cold with good watering. Best planted in late summer for fall crop.

- *St. Blaise:* Early spring planting under row covers; also thrives through the summer. Small upright heads; good variety for intensive gardens.

Butterhead Lettuces

Butterhead is preferred in Europe and catching on in North America. Soft heads consist of loosely folded leaves with delicate texture and flavor.

- *Arctic King:* Crisp and early-maturing; grows from early fall through winter for earliest spring crop in climates with winters that are not severe.

- *Bibb:* First American gourmet lettuce, bred by a Kentucky colonel, John Bibb, in the early 1900s; also called limestone lettuce. A spring lettuce maturing in sixty to seventy-five days.

- *Brune D'Hiver:* French heirloom. One of the hardiest; bronzed pale green. Delicate elongated head ready in spring from fall planting in open ground. Tolerates cool weather and turns rich red.

- *Burpee Bibb:* Small heads are slow to bolt, with loosely folded leaves. Heart blanches to golden yellow. Excellent for individual salads. Matures in about seventy-five days.

- *Buttercrunch:* Firm-headed, deep green variety with a buttery texture. Thick leaves are juicy and tender. Larger and more heat-tolerant than Bibb. Harvest throughout summer.

- *Capitane:* Dutch. Rosettes of large velvety leaves; vigorous growth for cool season and, once established, hot weather. Also a good choice for greenhouse growing.

- *Continuity:* Similar to Four Seasons; deeper in color and longer-lasting through dry summer weather.

- *Eline:* French. Summer (also adapted to spring and fall). Large; slow to bolt and tipburn; disease-resistant. Keeps a fresh green appearance in the garden.

- *Four Seasons:* Spring. Tender and crisp leaves; bright red outer leaves contrast with pink and cream interior.

- *Juliet:* Green and bronze-red leaves with satiny texture; tender, pale hearts. Matures in sixty days and will tolerate a variety of climates.

- *Kinemontpas:* French. Standard summer lettuce in France. Slow to bolt, pale green.

- *Mantilia:* French. Heat-tolerant midseason heads are dense and disease-resistant. Prized in southern France for retaining flavor in summer heat.

- *May King:* Early spring. Compact, tender head of pale green tinged with red; grow in the open or under covers.

- *Merveille des Quatre Saisons:* French. Huge, red-tipped leaves surrounding green hearts; introduced to the United States on the PBS series "The Victory Garden." Can be picked well into winter with some protection.

- *Nancy:* For spring and fall. Thick, crisp leaves make sturdy head that keeps well; large, dense heart. Disease-resistant.

- *North Pole:* Fall/winter. Pale green and very cold-hardy; adapted for overwintering under cover.

- *Orfeo:* Summer. Pale, soft head does well in summer heat.

- *Pirat:* Spring (midseason). Swiss. Pale green leaves mottled with bronze; also known as Sprenkel lettuce. Similar to Merveille des Quatre Saisons but more compact and heat-resistant.

- *Prado:* Late spring. Fast-growing, uniform, compact green head that resists bolting.

- *Red Riding Hood:* Summer. A red Boston type with good bolt resistance. Heads should be harvested at ½ to ¾ pound.

- *Rigoletto:* Summer; Dutch. Similar to Orfeo, with more glaucous leaf, and darker green color.

- *Sangria:* Spring and fall; summer in cooler areas and winter where frost-free. French. Rosy red color with smooth, thick, wavy leaves. Slow to bolt.

- *Voluma:* Spring. Dutch. Smooth-textured and resistant to disease.

- *Winter Marvel:* Fall/winter. Completely winter-hardy, even in Vermont. Produces large, pale green heads in early spring from fall planting.

Loose Leaf or Loose Head Lettuces

These plants form loose rosettes rather than heads. Individual leaves or the entire plant can be harvested.

- *Biondo Lisce*: Spring. Tender and quick-growing; can be cut as early as one month after seeding.

- *Black-Seeded Simpson*: Spring. One of the earliest lettuces; light green, juicy, and crispy; center leaves almost white.

- *Grand Rapids*: Spring. Light green leaves are tender and frilled; slow to bolt.

- *Green Ice*: Spring. Least bitter of all leaf lettuces; leaves are crinkled and dark green. Slow to bolt.

- *Lolla Rossa*: Spring. Italian. Densely ruffled, crinkly, crimson leaves, tapering to pale green hearts. Heat-tolerant. A related variety, pale green in color, is Lolla Biondo.

- *Oak Leaf*: Spring. Notched leaves are tender and sweet; tolerates hot weather.

- *Red Oak Leaf*: Spring. Shades of burgundy and cranberry, sweet flavor, and delicate texture.

- *Red Sails*: Spring. Fast-growing, heat-tolerant, extremely slow to bolt in comparison with other red leaf lettuces. Broad, open heads up to a foot across.

- *Rossa D'Amerique*: Spring. Italian. Pale green leaves tipped with red. Cut leaves for salad, or thin and let loose heads form.

- *Rossa di Trento*: Italian. Broad, savoyed, red-tipped leaves; for year-round growing in mild climates.

- *Royal Oak Leaf*: Spring. More defined oak-leaf shape than traditional Oak Leaf. Tolerates summer heat.

- *Royal Red*: Spring. Brilliant red; slower to reach full size, but good resistance to bolt and tipburn.

- *Ruby*: Spring. Bright green, frilled leaves shaded with intense red.

- *Salad Bowl*: Spring. Deeply lobed green leaves are easy to grow, heat-resistant. There is also a red-leaved form, Red Salad Bowl.

- *Slobolt*: Summer. Slowest-bolting green leaf lettuce. Pale green, frilly leaves; tolerant of tipburn.

- *Tango*: Spring. Deep green, heavily savoyed rosettes. Needs to be cut young; not very heat-tolerant.

- *Waldman's Dark Green*: Spring and fall best; also summer. Dark green, frilled, ruffled leaves form a loose, well-bunched rosette.

Crisphead Lettuces

Also called Batavian, iceberg, or French Crisp, these European favorites come in a variety of colors and shapes. Harvest individual sweet leaves, or let plants mature into big, crunchy, loose heads by thinning them early to stand a foot apart.

- *Anuenue*: Spring, summer, fall. Bright glossy green leaves around a large, well-packed heart.

- *Burpee's Iceberg*: Vigorous, hardy; medium-size heads with succulent hearts that blanch silver-white.

- *Canasta*: Spring, summer, fall. French. Shiny, puckered leaves tinged with red, forming a whorl. Resistant to bolt, tipburn, bottom rot.

- *Cocarde*: Spring. Red Oak Leaf type, with loose heads growing more than a foot across, or cut-and-come-again. Slow to bolt.

- *Crispino*: Spring. Early, dependable, with white interior; juicy, with good flavor.

- *Garnet*: Spring. Crisp, nonbitter, bright green with red tips. Leaves form attractive loose bunch.

- *Great Lakes*: Spring. Large, well-folded heads hold up well in warm weather.

- *Ithaca*: Spring. Improved iceberg type adapted for the Northeast.

- *Kristia*: French. Heat-tolerant with crisp, juicy leaves that can be harvested individually or allowed to mature into large, heavy heads.

- *Minetto*: Spring. Early, compact heads, dependable and crisp.

- *Reine des Glaces*: Spring. Deeply notched leaves, convoluted head of frosty green.

- *Rosy*: Spring. Small red iceberg, similar to Ithaca. Tolerant of bad conditions and slow to bolt.

- *Rouge Grenobloise*: Spring. French. Performs well in difficult conditions, with shiny, crunchy green and red leaves.

- *Victoria*: Spring, summer, fall, especially for summer. Heavy, upright, open head of crisp, sweet, juicy leaves. Long harvest period; resistant to bolting.

Baby Lettuces

Small heads 4 to 6 inches across save space in the garden and make perfect individual salads.

- *Baby Oak*: Spring. Loose leaf, one half to one third the size of regular Oak Leaf, and maturing nearly a week sooner.

- *Little Gem Mini Romaine*: English heirloom. Small heads with crisp leaves grow rapidly for succession sowing.

- *Rougette du Midi*: Fall/winter. Also known as Red Montpelier, a small red head good for baby lettuce or off-season cold-frame crops. Not for summer.

- *Rubens Dwarf Romaine*: Semi-dwarf, 12-inch heads of lavish color and full, sweet flavor.

- *Summer Baby Bibb*: Small, sturdy rosettes of tender, teardrop-shaped leaves.

- *Tom Thumb*: English heirloom. Mild and sweet favorite in cottage gardens.

Washing and Preparing Your Salad Greens

From the catalog of the Cook's Garden comes this wisdom:

Salad oil will not coat the leaves [of greens] if they are wet. Separate the leaves and wash thoroughly in cold water. Dry in a spinner or by letting them drip in a colander, then wrap lightly in soft absorbent towel and chill in the refrigerator. When storing washed greens, place loosely in a plastic bag and add a few single sheets of paper towel to absorb [extra] moisture. Loosely tie the end of the plastic bag. Before you add any dressing, mix the greens in the salad bowl with a tablespoon of olive oil and coat the surface of each leaf thoroughly. This keeps them from wilting in reaction to the vinegar and salt of the dressing.

Lettuce at a Glance

SOW INDOORS OR UNDER GLASS: 6 weeks before last frost.

GERMINATION: 7 to 14 days at 70°F.

DIRECT-SEED OUTDOORS: As soon as soil is dry enough to be worked.

PLANT OUT: After danger of hard frost.

SEED DEPTH: ¼ inch.

DISTANCE BETWEEN PLANTS: Thin cutting lettuce, 4 inches apart; butterhead, crisphead, and romaine, 8 to 14 inches apart.

SOIL: Nutrient-rich; pH 6.0 to 7.0.

SUNLIGHT: Full sun early in the day; give afternoon shade in high summer.

WATER: Keep moist.

FEEDING: Topdress weekly with compost, or water with compost tea.

COMPANION CROPS: Carrots, radishes, corn, tomatoes, onions, garlic.

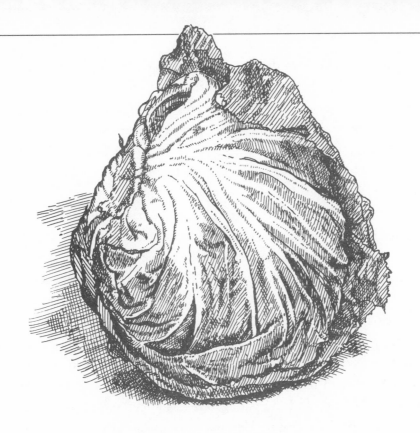

CHICORIES (RADICCHIO)

When some years ago a neighbor of mine gave me some seedlings
he called "Italian lettuce," I set out the transplants among my Silver
Queen corn and took a taste from time to time out of curiosity. As
the season advanced, the plants' bitterness was unendurable, so I pulled
them all up and gave them to my chickens. One plant, quite by
accident, survived the holocaust and evaded notice until September
when the corn harvest was complete. There stood an upright plant
looking not unlike a loose head of romaine, its tongue-shaped leaves
tingued with red. I snapped off a bit of leaf for a taste, and found it
was delicious. Some Italian lettuce! The plant was actually Treviso
chicory, also known as radicchio. I've been growing it ever since.

Until as recently as the late 1980s, you'd have done well to find
more than a variety or two of chicory in American seed catalogs.
Sugarhat was offered for greens, Magdeburg for producing roots to
grind and use as a coffee substitute, and, in some places, Witloff
chicory for forcing Belgian endive.

But then America discovered radicchio! These tight heads of red-purple leaves with dramatic and prominent white ribs and veins appeared first in salads in sophisticated restaurants. Soon radicchio could be found in growing numbers of supermarket produce departments at prices ranging anywhere from $3.99 to $6.99 per pound. Now many types of chicory or radicchio can be found in the salad gardens of America.

In fact, there are so many different types of plants within this interesting and varied genus that even experienced gardeners are likely to experience a bit of confusion at first. I've been growing a few of the radicchios for several years, and I must admit I've barely scratched the surface of understanding.

First, there are chicories grown for their leaves and there are those grown for their roots. Of the former there are green-leaved and red-leaved varieties, although the red-leaved plants actually remain green until cool fall weather turns them red. Of the reds, there are Verona, Treviso, and the variegated Castelfranco types—named for the towns of their origin. Verona varieties produce round heads on compact plants; Treviso and Castelfranco are larger and produce erect heads not unlike loose-headed romaine. Of the green-leaved varieties, there are cutting chicories (Spadona), spring chicories (Puntarella, Grumolo, Dentarella), and Sugarloaf; of these, Sugarloaf is most popular in this country.

Some chicories can be started in early spring for harvest when the plants are still tiny; other varieties, because their leaves are so bitter in hot weather, must be planted in midsummer for a very late autumn or early winter harvest—or, when protected over the winter, an early harvest the following spring. And still other chicories (certain of the reds and the famous Witloof) require forcing indoors if they're to be brought to table as an edible salad ingredient. But all these diverse chicories belong to a single species, *Cichorium intybus*.

To confuse matters still more, there's the closely related endive, a leafy crop of another species in the same genus. Is it to be considered a chicory at all just because of its botanical name (*Cichorium endivia*) or because of its titular association with Belgian endive, the forced gourmet chicon of the Witloof chicory root? Some catalogs say yes and some say no. I've listed endive separately to reduce confusion, but no matter what the thing is officially called, you're going to want to grow those curly and finely cut leaves which greengrocers like to call chicory, or these days, *frisée*. I also hope you'll try the broadleaf variety which the greengrocers call escarole.

My personal recommendation for the gardener unfamiliar with chicory is that you grow at least one of the round, red, heading radicchios (Verona types) newly developed for the burgeoning market. They never get bitter and are as easy to grow as lettuce from early spring onward. Success is guaranteed. And the first time you serve a salad with your own homegrown radicchio, your friends will definitely be impressed.

How to Grow Chicory

While it may be advisable to start some of the red-leaved Verona chicories (such as Giulio, Cesare, Silla, and Marina) indoors, they and others, including the green Sugarloaf, are just as easily direct-seeded in the garden from midspring to midsummer. Hot soil will retard germination, so be sure to keep your seedbed moist and as cool as you can manage. Use boards or even black plastic mulch over the bed until the seeds have germinated.

The young thinnings of all chicories are delicious in salads (though perhaps my tolerance for bitterness may be greater than yours), so don't worry if your seedlings are overcrowded. Thin plants every few days until they stand 5 to 6 inches apart (or 8 to 10 inches for the green-leaved Sugarloaf, which matures like romaine lettuce). Sugarloaf, by the way, is also excellent as a seedling crop if sown under cover—in a cold frame, indoors in pots on the windowsill, or under lights.

Some chicories grown on average and even poor soil do quite well, though many require—and all will surely benefit from—life in nutrient-rich soil. Keeping the soil from drying out and providing a bit of midseason shade will make for sweeter plants that do not bolt. Chicories are rarely attacked by insects or disease.

How to Harvest Chicory

Spring-sown red Treviso chicories can be harvested for their young leaves as soon as they're large enough to eat (2 to 3 inches long). Harvest can continue until hot weather arrives—when, with the exception of Giulio, Cesare, Silla, and Marina, the leaves become far too bitter to eat. Harvest young plants by cutting them right down to the ground. Thereafter, thin out plants to stand from 5 to 10 inches apart, depending upon the variety, and nurture them into the cooler days of early autumn.

Harvest the red Verona varieties Giulio, Cesare, Marina, and Silla when the heads are the size of baseballs and feel tight. The small, attractive heads stand an exceptionally long peak time in the garden, remaining crisp and tender even during the sweltering days of August. Cut the earliest heads an inch or two above ground level and you may be rewarded with new growth before the end of the season. Thereafter, cut heads flush with the soil.

Where winter temperatures drop below 10°F, you've got some choices if you want to bring the traditional Verona and Treviso types—originally intended for fall planting and spring harvesting in mild climates—to table.

First, you can cut back plants in early September and they will put out new heads by late October. If frost is predicted, cover the

RADICCHIO,
RED TREVISO

The Salad Lover's
GARDEN

plants. The heads will turn red only after the weather becomes consistently cool. If, as many radicchio cognoscenti prefer, you'd like to blanch the Verona heads, cover the bed with black plastic mulch. To blanch the hearts of the tall, upright Treviso plants, simply tie the leaves together with string.

Plants of both Treviso and Verona can also be brought indoors and forced in much the same way as Witloof is forced (see later). The only difference is that, when forcing red chicories, you leave the topgrowth in place and bring in the entire plant—top, root, and all—while with Witloof the leaves are snipped off.

I have no experience growing chicory in a region of mild winters, but for those of you who enjoy such luxury, I offer the following technique, which comes by way of English horticulturist Joy Larkcom, author of *The Salad Garden* (The Viking Press, 1984). Ms. Larkcom advises cutting back the head in late autumn, leaving a couple inches of stem. Then bury the plants in soil or ashes to a depth of about 8 inches. In spring, the newly sprouted heads down below will force themselves up through the darkness and emerge as tight, whitened, tender chicons, as they say, "to die for."

Sugarloaf chicory can be harvested for several weeks once the leaves are about 2 inches tall. In cold climates, getting the sweet-tasting romainelike heads to mature is tricky. You can try planting seeds earlier than the usual planting time in midspring, but if you don't provide shade for plants from the blazing heat of midsummer, they'll bolt almost as fast as spinach. Assuming you can bring them successfully through the heat, you will have to protect plants from frost just a few weeks later. The plants will need protection from even light frosts, because maturing Sugarloaf chicory is quite tender. For these reasons, no doubt, only a few seed catalogs offer green-leaved chicories.

There are other green-leaved chicories to try besides Sugarloaf, including Grumulo, Spadona, Catalogna (grown for its leafstalks and flowering shoots) and even wild chicory, which is sold in some catalogs. Space prohibits a detailed discussion of these lesser-known varieties, but growing instructions will come with your seed packets.

Salad Greens
and Herbs

RECOMMENDED VARIETIES
OF CHICORY

Round-headed Varieties

- *Alto:* Spring, summer, fall. Heavy and relatively larger heads, with good heat tolerance.

- *Augusto:* Mid- to late summer for fall harvest. Frost-tolerant; deep burgundy red.

- *Castelfranco:* Marbled red and white coloring; loose, slow-bolting heads. Plant in spring for midsummer harvest.

- *Cesare:* Early to midsummer planting. Italian. Burgundy-colored with white midribs; the tender leaves from loose heads.

- *Giulio:* Spring planting for summer harvest. Italian; first spring-planted radicchio, with small, solid red head.

- *Marina:* Sow seed from May to June; harvest from late summer through fall. Dark red heads; doesn't need cutting back before harvesting.

- *Medusa:* All cropping periods. Early variety with medium-size dark red heads.

- *Rossa di Verona or Red Verona:* Plant in summer for second growth in cold weather. Italian. Very cold-hardy, changing from green to red in cool weather.

- *Silla:* Early spring. Plant under row covers for deep red heads the size of tennis balls in early July.

Tall-headed Varieties

- *Early Treviso:* Mid-July seeding for September. Slow to bolt with late summer planting.

- *Palla Rossa:* Spring. Paler and larger than other radicchios.

- *Rossa di Treviso or Red Treviso:* Plant in summer for second growth in cold weather. Italian; elongated red heads for cold-weather harvest.

Green-headed Chicory

- *Pan di Zucchero, Pain de Sucre, or Sugarloaf:* Plant in midspring for late summer harvest. Forms a heavy, romaine-type head. Big green leaves are milder than those of most radicchios.

Cutting Chicory

- *Spadona:* Also known as dog's tongue chicory; smooth sword-shaped leaves grow vigorously. Sow every few weeks from early spring through summer for a continuous supply of salad leaves.

Spring Chicory

- *Ceriolo (Grumolo):* Low-growing rosette type, with small, 2-to 3-inch heads.

- *Dentarella:* Straight and succulent stems give this variety the alternate name of asparagus chicory.

- *Puntarella:* Twisted succulent stems are harvested about the same time as asparagus.

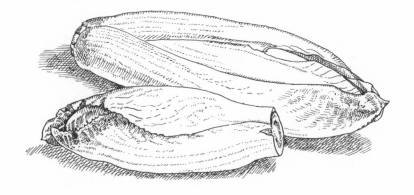

Belgian Endive

Perhaps the most exceptional salad ingredient is Belgian endive, the product of forcing the roots of Witloof chicory—a relatively simple process if you have the right conditions.

First you've got to grow the roots, which is accomplished by sowing seed in late spring to early summer and thinning the emerging plants to stand about 6 inches apart. Three dozen healthy roots provide plenty of Belgian endive for a family of salad lovers. By the way, feel free to harvest young leaves early in the season—they make excellent salad greens.

Dig the roots carefully after the first few light fall frosts. Trim the roots to a length of 8 inches, then stand them upright about 2 inches apart in buckets or boxes of dry sand or peat, leaving 4 inches or so from their crowns to the top of the storage container. For home use, storage containers should hold a maximum of a dozen roots each. Store the roots in your cool basement—where, we hope, the temperature remains below 60°F (the cooler the better, as long as the temperature stays above freezing) and the humidity is high. Let the roots rest for a month in the darkness.

To start the forcing process, water the storage medium and cover the roots with more sand, filling the containers right up to the top. This step is not necessary if forcing is done in the dark. In a month

87

*Salad Greens
and Herbs*

the tender chicons will have grown to a height of about 4 to 6 inches, at which time you can just snap them off and start preparing your salad.

After your first harvest, water the medium again and you should get a second harvest. You might even get a third.

CHICORIES AT A GLANCE

SOW INDOORS OR UNDER GLASS: Some red-leaved varieties can be started indoors, but most chicories can be direct-seeded outdoors.

GERMINATION: 14 days.

DIRECT-SEED OUTDOORS: From early spring onward, depending on variety.

PLANT OUT: Set out seedlings from midspring through midsummer.

SEED DEPTH: ¼ inch.

DISTANCE BETWEEN PLANTS: 8–10 inches.

SOIL: Deep, rich soil; pH 5.5 to 6.8.

SUNLIGHT: Full sun, generally. Plants appreciate partial shade in midseason.

WATER: Moderate, steady supply.

FEEDING: Unnecessary.

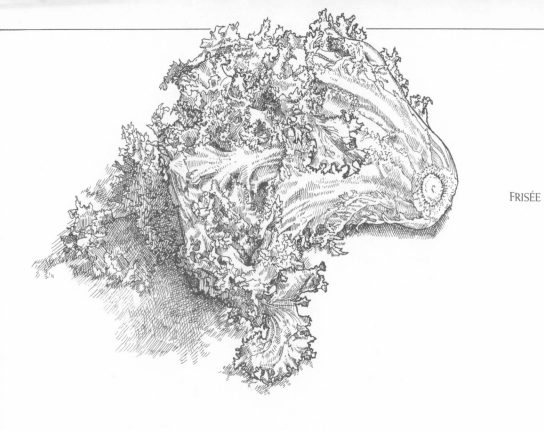

ENDIVE AND ESCAROLE

Endive and escarole are both chicories of the species *Cichorium endiva*. What distinguishes them from each other is the shape of their leaves. Endive (what is often called chicory in the supermarket) has finely cut, curly leaves, while escarole is a smooth, broadleaf variety.

In recent years, a more interesting form of endive called frisée has begun to appear in stores (at rather rarefied prices, I might add— usually between four and five dollars per pound). Cultivated for centuries in France, but only in relatively few American gardens, these smaller, more delicate heads than those normally sold as endive or chicory have magnificent flavor. Their nutty, buttery bitterness offsets the mild sweetness of lettuces.

The hearts of escarole are lovely in salads, their ribs lending a pleasant crunch, but the outer leaves are almost always too bitter to eat raw. Steamed for several minutes, however, and served with a dressing of extra virgin olive oil, fresh lemon juice, and a little salt, pepper, and garlic, they make a wonderful side dish to any meal.

ESCAROLE

How to Grow Endive

Both frisée and escarole should be planted quite early in the season.
You can sow seeds indoors for early transplanting or direct-sow in
the garden as soon as the soil can be worked. Sow in shallow drills
or broadcast, and cover with ½ inch of sifted compost. Thin plants
so they eventually stand about 9 inches apart. Succession sowings can
be made every three weeks through early summer. For seed sown
when the weather is already hot, you will have to provide continuous
even moisture or shade until germination occurs. And be advised that
the earlier-planted endives will become very bitter in hot weather
unless they are blanched as described later. Thinnings from your last
sown crop can be used in salads, leaving the remaining plants spaced
9 to 12 inches apart to mature in the cooler weather of autumn.

　　　As with all leaf crops, the faster endives grow the better, so
provide them with well-worked, richly composted soil and plenty of
moisture.

RECOMMENDED VARIETIES
OF ENDIVE AND ESCAROLE

Curly Endive or Frisée

- *Fin des Louviers:* French. Popular with specialty-market gardners.

- *Fine Curled:* Finely cut leaves can be cut singly or allowed to head up; also can be blanched.

- *Nina:* Long, smooth, deeply cut gray-green leaves. Mild and delicious; for early harvest.

- *Salad King:* Broader-leaved but curly; resistant to problems of cold, wet fall weather.

- *Très Fin Marchière:* French. Finely cut, lacy leaves; fast-growing. Mature heads are hand-size and easy to grow.

Broadleaf Endive or Escarole

- *Cornet d'Anjou:* Fall and spring. A heading escarole shaped like the mouth of a horn; should be blanched.

- *Nuvol:* Also known as Batavian endive, has large head and wavy, dark green, broad leaves. Self-blanching.

- *Sinco:* Cool season (late summer or fall); also overwinters. French. Big head with large leaves around closely bunched crunchy heart.

How to Care for Endive

Because endive has a tendency to bolt in the heat, your primary task will be to keep the soil cool by providing steady moisture and perhaps even a bit of shade. For this you can use a white bed sheet tied to low stakes or special plant-shading material available through most garden supply catalogs.

To fend off another of the natural tendencies of endive—to become bitter—you may choose to blanch the plants. They don't last long after being blanched, so do only a few at a time. The process will take about a week (longer in fall) and can be accomplished by covering the mature plant with a clay pot, a plastic bucket, or anything else that will keep out sunlight. Blanching presents a danger of rot and mold, so begin the blanching process on a hot, dry day to be certain the leaves are dry. Any covering you use must also be able to exclude rain.

How to Harvest Endive

Most endives take from seventy to ninety days to mature. Early sowings that would do most of their maturing in extremely hot temperatures might be better used as cutting crops. Whenever the leaves are 3 to 4 inches high, cut them down to within an inch of the ground and they will come back to be cut again. Later plantings should be left to mature in fall, when cooler temperatures will abate their bitter flavor.

ENDIVE AT A GLANCE

SOW INDOORS OR UNDER GLASS: 6 weeks before last frost, then again in midseason to ensure germination for a fall harvest.

GERMINATION: 10 to 14 days.

DIRECT-SEED OUTDOORS: As soon as soil can be worked, and successively every 3 weeks through early summer.

PLANT OUT: In early spring.

SEED DEPTH: ½ inch.

DISTANCE BETWEEN PLANTS: 9 to 12 inches.

SOIL: Rich, well worked; ph 6.0 to 7.0.

SUNLIGHT: Likes a little shade in the heat of summer.

WATER: Keep soil moist.

FEEDING: Unnecessary if soil is sufficiently rich.

SPINACH

After lettuce and chicory, spinach follows as a major player in the
great American salad. Where spring lettuces are slender and delicate,
spinach is strapping and robust. Thick and lustrous, it can put forth
a rush of luxuriant, glossy growth and be gone from the garden before
the tomatoes have ripened a single fruit. And if you wind up planting
more than you can handle for fresh eating, versatile spinach, unlike
most other leafy salad crops, may be blanched and frozen for later
use as a delicious cooked vegetable.

Of all the leaf vegetables, spinach may well be the heaviest
feeder. It requires soil rich in nutrients and a steady supply of moisture
if it is to perform as it should—with rapid, unimpeded growth from
germination through maturity.

Years ago, I was impressed by an article in which the gardener
described raising a prolific crop of Agway thirty-day hybrid spinach
in virtually pure uncomposted cow manure. The concept was on the
one hand totally gross (there is considerable romance in manure, and
I mean this seriously, but little of it is attached to the stuff when it

is freshly manufactured), and on the other hand entirely logical. Having access to an unlimited supply from a nearby farm, I duplicated the experiment on a small section of my garden (for obvious olfactory reasons) and it worked quite well.

Then, of course, it was discovered (or perhaps it had been discovered quite some time earlier but only recently reported) that the use of fresh manure on leaf crops is neither wise nor healthful. The plants absorb great quantities of the nitrate salts which are in plentiful supply in manure. I now use only aged and less malodorous manure. This provides an equally continuous and plentiful supply of nitrogen-giving materials which allows spinach to rocket the way it's supposed to.

Sow spinach in shallow drills about ¼ inch deep as soon in the season as the soil can be worked. If your soil leans to the heavy side, cover the seeds with sifted compost or peat moss. The fine covering will prevent the clay soil from crusting over and making it difficult for seedlings to emerge. Keep the seedbed moist until germination is complete, and right on through spinach's growing season.

For a steady supply of young spinach, resow every ten days or so. Be advised, however, that spinach seed germinates poorly once soil temperatures rise above 75°F. One good trick to improve germination in midsummer is to keep the soil cool by covering the newly planted and watered seedbed with wide boards until germination occurs. Tricks and tips notwithstanding, when the weather gets hot, spinach wants to bolt to seed and usually does. Sow again in late summer for a fall harvest, but keep the soil cool if you expect decent seed germination.

How to Care for Spinach

As with any direct-seeded crop, a tendency exists for spinach seedlings to be overcrowded. Thin periodically until plants stand 3 to 6 inches apart, depending on how large you want them to be (the farther apart the plants, the larger they will grow). Water freely with manure or compost tea, and topdress with compost or aged manure when plants are 3 inches tall.

Leaf miners are occasionally a problem, burrowing between leaf surfaces and into stems and disfiguring plants. Keeping the area weed-free will remove hosts that attract the parent flies, and cultivating the soil will simultaneously kill pupae. If you suspect leaf miners, inspect leaves for egg clusters and scrape them off. Covering the row with cheesecloth or Reemay will prevent flies from laying eggs.

Downy mildew, a disease spread by windblown spores, creates yellowish and brownish spots on older leaves, which dry, curl, and die. Keep plants well thinned to provide adequate air circulation, and remove any affected plants immediately and burn them. Plant varieties resistant to mildew.

How to Harvest Spinach

Plant maturity, as I've mentioned on numerous earlier occasions, is a relative thing in the salad garden. That is, a crop is mature when *you* decide to eat it, not when the seed catalog says it's time to harvest. That said, it should be noted that various spinach cultivars do take differing amounts of time to come to maturity, that is, full size. The range is from about thirty to fifty days. Peculiarly, Tyee—first introduced by Johnny's Selected Seeds, and one of my favorite varieties—is listed at forty-two days in Johnny's catalog and fifty-three days in Stokes. Maturity is totally subjective for salad crops: Just pick your spinach when you want to eat it.

Like all leaf crops, spinach is a cut-and-come-again green. When you want some fresh spinach, take a sharp knife out to the garden and cut down a swath of it, leaving about an inch of stem remaining. If really hot weather holds off, you may get up to three cuttings from the same bed before the crop bolts. Harvested in the cool hours of the morning, washed, and then chilled, spinach will make a hearty lunch or evening salad. Thinly slice a little sweet red onion, add a few wedges of hard-boiled egg and some warm, crisp bacon (if meat is to your liking), and shower it all with a raspberry vinaigrette.

*Salad Greens
and Herbs*

SPINACH SUBSTITUTES

Unless you are able to shade your spinach in hot weather, it will usually bolt to seed in early summer, leaving you without spinach until your fall crop is ready. Here are three additional plants which will endure sultry summer weather and favor your salads with acceptable spinach alternatives.

Amaranth Tricolor: This double-threat salad vegetable, used for both its leaves and its stems, happens also, with its red, green, and reddish purple tinted leaves, to be quite beautiful. Start seeds indoors for midspring transplanting, or sow directly in the garden when the soil is warm and the danger of lingering frosts has passed. Amaranth tastes best when grown quickly, so make sure the soil is rich and the supply of water steady. Thin plants to stand 6 inches apart, and harvest leaves when plants are young— about 4 inches tall. The plants' seedheads are lovely, but don't let them come to maturity, as they produce zillions of seeds that will freely self-sow.

Orach: Known also as mountain spinach, this delicately flavored leaf crop strongly resembles the common garden weed lamb's-quarters (which, by the way, also makes delectable salad greens when young).

Orach comes in green, red, and yellow varieties. When planted in good soil (you should plant orach in succession from spring through early summer) orach of any color will reach a height of 6 feet. If you decide to let it grow, keep it on the north or east end of your garden, where you would also do well to interplant lettuce seedlings in hot weather. Space orach plants to stand 8 to 12 inches apart, and begin harvest when they are in the range of 4 to 8 inches tall. Remove flower stalks when they appear, and keep plants cut back to generate growth of tender new leaves. Orach can also be cooked. Be warned, however, that red orach will run its color onto everything else in the pot, like beets.

New Zealand spinach: Named for the location of its discovery by the crew of Captain James Cook, this pseudo-spinach is pretty close to the real thing in terms of flavor. A perennial in its native clime, it is grown in temperate climates as a half-hardy annual. Sow seeds in midspring, and keep well watered throughout the growing season. Harvest outer leaves to stimulate tender new growth, which makes the best contribution to the salad bowl.

The Salad Lover's
GARDEN

RECOMMENDED VARIETIES
OF SPINACH

- *Avon Hybrid:* Quick-growing; large succulent leaves are semi-crinkled, easy to clean.

- *Bloomsdale Long-Standing:* Heavy-yielding with very crinkled leaves; slow to bolt.

- *Estivato:* Seed from mid-April to mid-July; harvest mid-June to Labor Day. Heat-tolerant; open-pollinated.

- *Giant Nobel Hybrid:* Early and fast-growing; tolerant of tipburn.

- *Indian Summer:* Spring, summer, and fall crops. Dark green, upright; slow to bolt.

- *Italian Summer:* Summer. High-yielding plants grow well throughout season, with good bolt resistance.

- *Melody Hybrid:* Large, semierect plants are disease-resistant.

- *Nordic:* Early summer. Dutch. Smooth crisp leaves with delicate flavor.

- *Sputnik:* Plant early spring to late summer. Three-season hybrid; mildew-resistant, with large green leaves.

- *Tyee:* Spring and summer harvest. Dark green leaves; bolt-resistant with vigorous growth.

- *Wolter:* Needs cool weather. Dutch. Disease-resistant, with fine flavor.

SPINACH AT A GLANCE

SOW INDOORS OR UNDER GLASS: Best for outdoor planting.

GERMINATION: 10 to 14 days at soil temperatures of 55 to 75°F. Keep seedbed moist during early heat waves or germination will be poor.

DIRECT-SEED OUTDOORS: As soon as soil can be worked.

SEED DEPTH: ¼ inch.

DISTANCE BETWEEN PLANTS: 3 to 6 inches.

SOIL: Rich, well fertilized; pH 6.0 to 7.5.

SUNLIGHT: Full sun.

WATER: Keep soil moist.

FEEDING: Topdress with compost, or water the plants with manure or compost tea.

COMPANION CROPS: Strawberries.

ARUGULA

Known as rocket, rocket salad, roquette, rucola, and rugola, this Mediterranean native, long thought to be an aphrodisiac and therefore an excellent plate mate for the opposing force of lettuce, has become extremely fashionable in the United States over the last decade, both as a solo salad ingredient and as a pungent addition to the general salad bowl. This strong-flavored plant will grow leaves more than 2 feet in length, if allowed to, though only a fool with a strong stomach would think of eating them at that stage.

How to Grow Arugula

The best arugula is grown very early in spring under cover, or later in summer for a fall harvest. Succession sowings can be made throughout the season, but the crops grown in cool weather will be most welcome on the table. Sow seed in shallow drills, or broadcast in a small patch for a cutting crop. A single broadcast planting may yield up to four or five cuttings. Space plants (or thin to) 6 inches apart.

How to Care for Arugula

If the speedy growth essential for raising plants of superior quality is to occur, your main focus is to see to it before planting that the soil is well manured or supplied with compost. Thereafter, keep the soil moist; forget plants grown on dry soil, as they become too strongly flavored to eat. As for insect and disease problems, arugula is rarely bothered.

ARUGULA

The Salad Lover's
GARDEN

How to Harvest Arugula

Arugula, like lettuce and spinach, is an excellent cut-and-come-again salad crop, yielding many cuttings from a single sowing. Cut in bunches when leaves are 2 to 3 inches long, or pull entire plants. Left to flower and go to seed, arugula will self-sow freely—so grow a few for your own seed and discard all other plants once they've bolted.

ARUGULA AT A GLANCE

SOW INDOORS OR UNDER GLASS: In late winter or very early spring for spring cutting.

GERMINATION: 14 days.

DIRECT-SEED OUTDOORS: As soon as ground can be worked in early spring, and in succession every few weeks throughout the season.

SEED DEPTH: ½ inch.

DISTANCE BETWEEN PLANTS: 6 inches.

SOIL: Rich; pH 6.0 to 7.0.

SUNLIGHT: Full sun.

WATER: Keep soil evenly moist.

FEEDING: Unnecessary in rich soil.

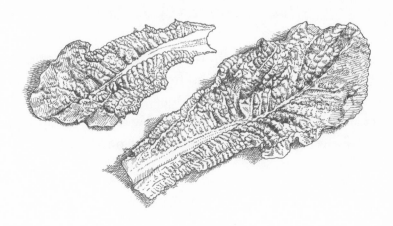

CELTUCE

Celtuce is one of those hybrid plants which comes by its name via the empirical route: The way it is used determines how it is named. The leaves are used like lettuce and the stems like celery. Not surprisingly, then, and by way of a similar naming strategy, this double-duty salad crop is also known as stem lettuce and asparagus lettuce. Descriptive nomenclature notwithstanding, you'll find it noteworthy that celtuce is in fact a variety of lettuce (*Lactuca sativa*), though of another group from our standard head and leaf varieties.

Picked young, the burly romaine-look-alike leaves are crisp and sweet in salads. As the season advances, quit harvesting leaves and wait until the stalks are ready (see "How to Harvest Celtuce," later).

How to Grow Celtuce

Since botanically it is a lettuce, celtuce should be grown as a lettuce. That is to say, plant it in well-worked rich soil early in the season. Make successive sowings for midseason supply and again in late summer for a fall harvest.

Start seeds indoors for the earliest crop, and set out plants in the garden as early as the danger of heavy frost is past. If you truly love your celtuce, prepare a bed in the fall and mulch it for the winter.

Pull back the mulch in early spring and set out your indoor-grown and well-hardened celtuce plants. Less passionate gardners can just wait until the soil is workable in spring, then sow seeds directly in the garden in very shallow drills or broadcast in wide beds. Barely cover the seeds with sifted sphagnum moss, just enough to exclude light. Germination occurs in seven to ten days. Start thinning when plants have their first set of true leaves, and keep it up until plants are about 10 to 12 inches apart.

How to Care for Celtuce

As you do for lettuce, make sure to keep the soil of your celtuce bed moist and well fortified with nutrients by way of a manure or compost topdressing every couple of weeks and an occasional watering with manure or compost tea. The major danger to celtuce is from slugs, which can be lured under boards in the row to escape the sun's heat, scooped up, and destroyed.

How to Harvest Celtuce

Thinnings can be used in salads, of course, but your first heavy harvest won't be for about a month. Simply strip off as many leaves as you need. As for the stem, that will be ready to harvest two months later. What you're looking for is the tender and tasty inner core of the stalk, which can be sliced or julienned and tossed into the salad. Cut the stalks at ground level, or pull up the plants entirely. Throw the old, bitter leaves on the compost or to your livestock, and then skin the stem until you arrive at the succulent heart. Eaten raw with salad, or steamed and served with a light butter sauce, the stem is a major delicacy.

CELTUCE AT A GLANCE

SOW INDOORS OR UNDER GLASS: 6 weeks before the last frost.

GERMINATION: 7 to 10 days.

DIRECT-SEED OUTDOORS: As soon as ground can be worked, in late spring for a midseason crop, then again in late summer for fall greens.

SEED DEPTH: ¼ inch.

DISTANCE BETWEEN PLANTS: 10 to 12 inches.

SOIL: Rich soil; pH 6.0 to 6.8.

SUNLIGHT: Full sun.

WATER: Moderate supply; about 1 inch per week.

FEEDING: Topdress with manure or compost or water with manure tea every two weeks.

The Salad Lover's
GARDEN

CHARD

Most commonly known as Swiss chard, this relative of the beet is often considered a substitute for spinach—not fresh spinach, mind you, but cooked. This is an important distinction, as Swiss chard, unless picked very young or forced, is not a salad standout. When buying chard seeds, select the varieties Argentata, Paros, and Rhubarb or Ruby Red. You may also find chard listed as perpetual spinach or spinach beet.

How to Grow Chard

Chard requires well-worked soil containing lots of compost if it is to do well. Broadcast seeds or sow in shallow drills in wide rows early in spring, spacing seeds about an inch apart. Seeds will germinate in ten to fourteen days, depending upon conditions. Once the seedlings are up and going strong, start thinning until plants eventually stand 6 inches apart. Sow again in midsummer for a fall crop.

How to Care for Chard

Care for chard in much the same way as you would spinach. Keep the soil moist, pull any weeds in the area, and mulch the soil· to conserve moisture. When flower stalks appear, snip them off. Occasionally slugs are a problem, so set traps in the rows. It's also not a bad idea to pull back your mulch every few days to see if slugs have collected there. When you find them, you know what to do.

103

*Salad Greens
and Herbs*

How to Harvest Chard

Your first harvest will, of course, be from early thinnings. Thereafter, strip each plant of its outside leaves and it will continue to produce tender new leaves in the center. When the outside leaves start to lose their appeal, go for the heart leaves. And for a special chard treat, try forcing the plant right out in the garden, as follows: Cut the plant right down to within 1 inch of the soil surface. Cover the small stump with 6 inches or so of soil and water well. Within several days, a new, tight bud will begin to emerge from the stump. Feel for it gently, Wait until it just begins to emerge from the soil and snap it off. The compact chicon makes an interesting salad green.

CHARD AT A GLANCE

SOW INDOORS OR UNDER GLASS: Not an indoor starter.

GERMINATION: 10 to 14 days.

DIRECT-SEED OUTDOORS: In early spring, then again in mid to late summer for fall crop.

SEED DEPTH: ¾ inch.

DISTANCE BETWEEN PLANTS: 6 to 8 inches.

SOIL: Rich; pH 5.8 to 6.5.

SUNLIGHT: Full sun.

WATER: Moderate supply.

FEEDING: Apply compost topdressing every 2 to 3 weeks.

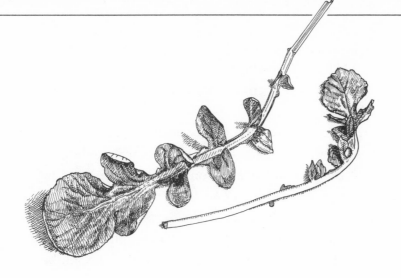

CRESSES

Three types of cress are available to salad gardeners: garden cress, upland cress, and watercress, all members of the Cruciferae (the cabbage family). Garden cress, also known in some circles as peppergrass, is a hot-tasting plant whose leaves add a pleasant tang to salads. Upland cress and watercress share a similar flavor, different from garden cress, but still rather peppery; they make wonderful solo salads with a variety of dressings, from a simple lemon and oil to some of the heavier cheese dressings—under which they still manage to hold their strong, but pleasant, flavor.

How to Grow Cresses

You can grow garden cress and upland cress indoors all year long as seedling crops. Out in the garden, they can be planted just as thickly in small patches and resown every three weeks or so for a steady supply. Both cresses prefer rich soil that retains moisture well. Broadcast seeds in wide rows and cover with ¼ inch of light soil. Seeds will germinate in about ten days.

Watercress is a perennial, though it requires conditions very close to those of its native habitat to perform in that capacity. In recent

105

*Salad Greens
and Herbs*

years I've grown watercress only for the fun of it, as I have more than I can possibly handle growing in a stream that runs through a hedgerow at the back of my property. I must admit I prefer the wild to the domesticated kind.

Start your watercress indoors by suspending supermarket-bought plants in water until the stems root. Then set the rooted stems outdoors in soil that remains moist all season long—beside a stream is ideal. Lacking a stream or any other body of running water, try planting watercress in clay pots and setting the pots in pans of water. You can also grow watercress from seed in the garden, but it must be planted in a spot that is perpetually wet. Broadcast in moist soil but do not cover, as the seed requires light to germinate.

How to Care for Cresses

If your soil is rich, the single most important task you face in bringing in high-quality cress is to provide ample, steady moisture to all of your cresses. If the soil dries out and gets hot, you might as well toss the cress to the chickens, because nobody else will want to eat these too-peppery greens.

Thin the plants to stand 6 inches apart, and mulch deeply to conserve moisture and keep the soil cool. If flower stalks appear, snap them off. Garden cress or upland cress left in the garden over winter will probably survive even severe conditions and, being biennials, will put out new growth in the spring.

If you're growing watercress in pots, be certain that you keep them in a lightly shaded area and change the water frequently—daily in very hot weather. You'll be rewarded when the crop comes in.

How to Harvest Cress

Garden cress is harvested as a cut-and-come-again crop, especially in the cool weather at either end of the growing season. Expect several cuttings in spring before the plants bolt to seed.

The small, central leaves of upland cress are both the tenderest and the best-flavored, so pick them in bunches as you need them. You can even cut the entire plants and they will make new growth.

Cut the outer leaves of watercress as you need them. You must make your harvests before the weather gets hot and the plants grow tall and less edible.

CRESSES AT A GLANCE

SOW INDOORS OR UNDER GLASS: Watercress can be started from cuttings and rooted in water before planting out. Garden and upland cress can be sown in pots on the windowsill as seedling crops; otherwise, direct-seed outdoors.

GERMINATION: 7 to 10 days.

DIRECT-SEED OUTDOORS: Early in spring and every 3 weeks through midsummer.

PLANT OUT: Set out watercress plants after threat of frost.

SEED DEPTH: ¼ inch.

DISTANCE BETWEEN PLANTS: 6 inches.

SOIL: Light, rich, moist; pH 6.5 to 7.5.

SUNLIGHT: Prefers some shade.

WATER: Steady supply for upland and garden cress; watercress needs running water or, when planted in pots, pans of water beneath.

FEEDING: Not necessary in rich soil.

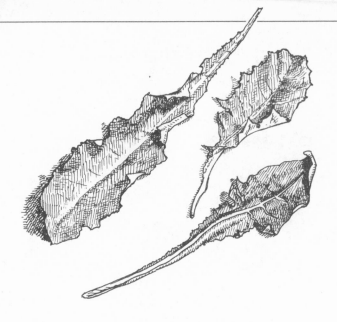

DANDELION

My earliest spring salads consist of young and wild dandelion, chicory, and watercress leaves with a little herbed goat cheese and a mild vinaigrette. The deeply cut dandelion leaves are tender and slightly bitter; they are best eaten young—the more mature they become, the more bitter they are.

Domestic dandelion, also a perennial, has all the wonderful flavor of the wild, with the added benefit of lasting longer in peak condition. However, once the plants enter truly warm weather, they require blanching.

Recommended varieties include Ameliore, Catalogna Special, and Mauser's Trieb.

How to Grow Dandelion

Nothing could be simpler than growing domestic dandelion. Sow indoors early in spring, or direct-seed in wide beds of well-drained soil containing lots of compost. Cover seed with ¼ inch of light soil or sifted compost, and allow ten to fourteen days for germination. Eventually, thin plants so they stand 12 inches apart.

The only vexing issue in cultivating dandelions is the risk you run in their taking over the garden. My suggestion is that you grow dandelion among perennial herbs or flowers, or, better yet, give them their own space where, if they spread, they will cause you no concern.

How to Care for Dandelion

Dandelion Responsibility Number One is to pick off all flower buds as they appear, stems and all. This accomplishes two very crucial ends: it allows the plants to concentrate their strength on producing leaves instead of flowers, and you avoid the possibility of profligate self-sowing (remember all the fuzzy wind-sown seeds?). Don't throw the flowers away; they are excellent when steamed with greens that have become too bitter to be eaten raw. And, if you have enough of them, you can make dandelion wine.

Otherwise, normal garden maintainance with keep dandelions quite happy. Don't let the soil dry out or the quality of the plants will decline. Like their wild cousins, domestic dandelions are seldom troubled by insects or disease. Slugs will sometimes be a problem, but a few traps will corral them.

How to Harvest Dandelion

Thinnings are your first harvest, of course, and can be used with wonderful results in salads. Take a fairly light harvest of early leaves from your newly established plants; a major cropping early in the first season might weaken these young perennials. As summer heads to a close, however, the plants will have made sufficient root growth to allow for blanching and heavier harvesting.

To blanch dandelion, cover the plants with flowerpots, making sure to plug the drainage holes to keep water out. Some gardeners prefer to dig entire plants and bring them indoors to blanch, though I have never tried this method. Some gardeners, this time including

*Salad Greens
and Herbs*

myself, dig roots for forcing, just as we do with Witloof chicory. Roots can also be dug, dried, roasted, and ground for a coffee substitute.

DANDELION AT A GLANCE

SOW INDOORS OR UNDER GLASS: 6 weeks before last frost.

GERMINATION: 10 to 14 days.

DIRECT-SEED OUTDOORS: As soon as soil can be worked; try again in late summer.

SEED DEPTH: ¼ inch.

DISTANCE BETWEEN PLANTS: 12 inches.

SOIL: Average soil; pH 5.8 to 6.5.

SUNLIGHT: Full sun.

WATER: Water deeply, especially during dry spells.

FEEDING: Unnecessary.

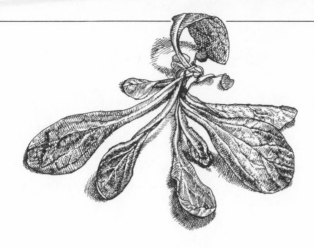

MÂCHE

Mâche (pronounced *mash*), known in this country until very recently
as corn salad, is a mild, nutty-flavored green that will grow all season
long and not become bitter, even after it has gone to seed. Being
narrow-leaved and low-growing, mâche, particularly late-sown crops
of it, may be interplanted with more widely spaced fall plantings of
cabbage or broccoli. And in areas where winters are severe, it can be
protected from snow by cloches and harvested in the cold months.
Good varieties include Coquille, D'Etemps, Elan, Piedmont, and Vit.

Mâche also grows wild, and once you've learned to identify it,
it's a good idea to make a habit of foraging for it in the fall, early
winter, and early spring when the snow is off the ground.

How to Grow Mâche

It is best to start mâche as early in spring as possible, either sown in
shallow drills or broadcast over a small patch. It prefers rich soil with
plenty of compost and manure, though it will perform admirably in
average soil as well. Make succession sowings throughout the season,
but be aware that because mâche seed is slower to germinate in warm
weather, you'll have to keep the soil moist during later sowings. The
effort will be worth it, for fall-maturing mâche is magnificent. Thin
plants to stand 4 inches apart.

*Salad Greens
and Herbs*

How to Care for Mâche

Mâche is very simple to grow. As with most leaf crops, your greatest concern is to supply it with abundant water. If slugs are not a problem in your garden, try mulching the plants with straw or grass clippings to conserve moisture. Apparently unattractive to pests and diseases, your mâche should provide you with no difficulty on that score either.

How to Harvest Mâche

Another of mâche's great qualities is its omniharvestability, if you know what I mean. It can be cut at the seedling stage early on; then, a couple of weeks later, you can harvest individual leaves. Finally, you may wait six to eight weeks for full plants, then slice off the heads at ground level and wait for new growth, which will come very soon.

MÂCHE AT A GLANCE

SOW INDOORS OR UNDER GLASS: Not an indoor starter.

GERMINATION: 10 to 14 days.

DIRECT-SEED OUTDOORS: As soon as soil can be worked, and every two weeks for a steady supply.

SEED DEPTH: ½ inch.

DISTANCE BETWEEN PLANTS: 4 inches.

SOIL: Rich pH 5.8 to 6.5.

SUNLIGHT: Full sun.

WATER: Moderate supply.

FEEDING: Unnecessary if soil is rich.

COMPANION CROPS: Late brassicas, corn, onions.

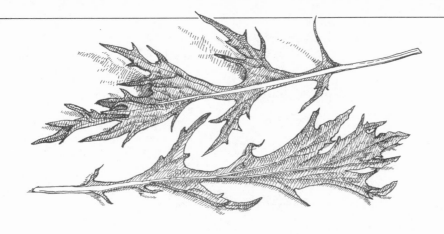

MUSTARD

It was not so very long ago that garden mustard was grown principally as a potherb in Southern gardens. Of course, many knowledgeable salad-loving gardeners have long been acquainted with the pleasure of eating young mustard leaves and flower stems, and they have begun to spread the word. That knowledge, along with a more accepting American palate—one willing to experiment with stronger flavors— accounts for mustard's becoming an ever more popular green, even in the North.

How to Grow Mustard

Keeping a family supplied with mustard all season long is simple, especially with some of the slower-to-bolt varieties such as Mizuna and Giant Red. Being a brassica, mustard, like cabbage, broccoli, and its other relatives, tends to like cool weather. Plant as early in the spring as you can get into the garden. Of course, mustard can be planted throughout the season.

Broadcast seeds or sow in shallow drills in wide rows, covering the seeds with ¼ inch of light soil or sifted compost. Because the seeds are very tiny and almost impossible to handle with any measure of control, try mixing them with a little sand and sprinkle the mixture as evenly as you can. Seedlings emerge in ten to fourteen days.

113

Salad Greens and Herbs

How to Care for Mustard

Thin your mustard patch so plants are eventually 4 to 6 inches apart. Keeping the bed moist throughout the growing season will ensure a milder-flavored ingredient for your salads. Fortunately, mustard is rarely bothered by diseases or insects, although aphids, flea beetles, and sometimes even slugs can be a problem. Soap sprays and traps will help you eliminate these pests if they show up.

How to Harvest Mustard

Your first mustard harvest will come from the inevitable thinnings of the newly germinated patch. Tossed into a salad at this stage, these delicate seedlings have only a hint of the peppery flavor they will develop later on.

Mustard is a wonderful cut-and-come-again crop, so you can harvest as much as you need for a salad by shearing off a bunch of leaves close to the ground, much as you would with loose leaf lettuce or spinach. Mustard is ideal for salads when the plants reach a height of 4 to 6 inches. Expect four or five cuttings this way, particularly with those varieties which are reluctant to bolt.

Flowering mustards include several varieties of pak choi and are generally listed under Chinese cabbage in seed catalogs (if available at all). They produce lovely flowers atop tender shoots, both of which are delicious in salads, especially when the plants are still young. Don't eat them raw when they get tough, but instead try steaming them with your mature mustard leaves.

RECOMMENDED VARIETIES
OF MUSTARD

- *English White*: A delightful English heirloom variety, serves best as a salad green when planted every few weeks and harvested when leaves are young.

- *Fordhook Fancy*: Plumelike leaves on compact plants are slow to bolt but should be harvested young.

- *Giant Red*: This Japanese variety has large purple-tinged leaves and should be harvested when plants are 6 inches tall. Pleasantly pungent flavor becomes bitter when plants get large.

- *Green Wave*: This fairly hot mustard should be used sparingly in salads. Stands well without bolting, but taller growth is more suitable for steaming than for salads.

- *Miike Purple*: This Japanese variety with purple-veined leaves has a definite peppery taste, so use sparingly in salads and harvest young leaves.

- *Mizuna or Kyona*: My favorite mustard of all. Leaves are deeply cut and plumelike; they are just mustardy enough to provide salads with a light zing. Plants stand well even in heat, but should be reseeded for a fall crop.

- *Osaka Purple*: Another favorite of mine, this showy Japanese mustard has red-purple leaves with white veins; it not only tastes good in salads but looks good, too.

- *Tendergreen*: Somewhat milder than Fordhook Fancy, this quick-growing American mustard has broad, smooth leaves.

MUSTARD AT A GLANCE

GIANT RED MUSTARD

SOW INDOORS OR UNDER GLASS: Not an indoor starter.

GERMINATION: 10 to 14 days.

DIRECT-SEED OUTDOORS: From early spring to late summer.

SEED DEPTH: ¼ inch.

DISTANCE BETWEEN PLANTS: 4 to 6 inches.

SOIL: Average; pH 6.0 to 6.8.

SUNLIGHT: Full sun.

WATER: Steady, moderate supply.

FEEDING: Unnecessary in reasonably rich soil.

*Salad Greens
and Herbs*

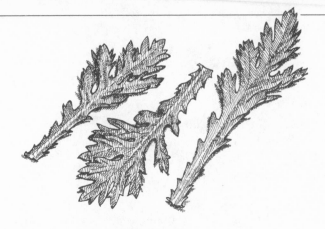

SHUNGIKU

You won't find shungiku in many catalogs, but I advise you to try. This easy-to-grow plant, known also as edible or garland chrysanthemum, crown daisy, and chop suey greens, is a salad bowl sleeper. Young leaves can be added to salads for a delicious and uniquely piquant flavor; when the small, lemon yellow flowers appear, they can also be tossed into the salad. Left to their own devices, the plants will grow 4 feet tall and will quickly go to seed.

How to Grow Shungiku

Broadcast seeds or sow in shallow drills in wide rows, covering seed with ¼ inch of fine, light soil. Seeds will germinate in ten to fourteen days. Shungiku will do well even in poor soil, but it does best, in my experience, when grown in compost-rich soil that retains moisture. Thin plants to stand 4 inches apart. Sow seed again in late summer for a fall harvest when, like a true chrysanthemum, it will brave many a hard frost before succumbing to winter.

How to Care for Shungiku

There is not much to caring for this Oriental green beyond standard garden maintenance. Keep the weeds down and the soil moist, and apply mulch for water conservation. Aphids and leaf miners are occasional attackers, though I've never seen them in my crops of shungiku. If aphids show up in yours, try soap and hot pepper sprays. For leaf miners, find egg cases, scrape them off the undersides of the leaves, and destroy; cover plants to keep parent flies from laying eggs again. Soil cultivation kills leaf miner pupae, so run the hoe around plants regularly.

How to Harvest Shungiku

When plants are 4 to 6 inches tall, harvest individual leaves or, if you prefer, cut the plant just above ground level and it will regrow if you haven't damaged the root in the process. Harvest flowers when young for salads; later they can be used as garnish and even pickled. Of course, the leaves can be used anytime in stir-fry dishes, a treat which should not be missed.

SHUNGIKU AT A GLANCE

SOW INDOORS OR UNDER GLASS: Can be sown indoors, but grows quickly when sown directly in the garden.

GERMINATION: 10 to 14 days.

DIRECT-SEED OUTDOORS: In early spring and then again in late summer for fall crop.

SEED DEPTH: ¼ inch.

DISTANCE BETWEEN PLANTS: 4 inches.

SOIL: Average; pH 6.0 to 7.0.

SUNLIGHT: Full sun to light shade.

WATER: Moderate supply.

FEEDING: Unnecessary except in poor soil.

In my second garden ever, I planted what I called a salad bed, in which I interplanted several kinds of lettuce, onions, and radishes. The idea was to go to one spot in the garden to pick a salad, rather than roaming here and there every evening. What I had inadvertently stumbled upon was the concept of mesclun, though my mixture, I admit, was a simple one.

If you've done any reading on the art of salad gardening or salad making, you've no doubt run across the French term *mesclun,* or the Italian *misticanza* and *saladini,* all of which mean a mixture of salad greens. Nowhere have I heard a simpler but more eloquent explanation of this time-honored European tradition than the one offered by Rosalind Creasy in her wonderful book called *Cooking from the Garden* (Sierra Club Books, 1989), which I paraphrase here: When it comes to growing salads, she says, you can either mix the greens in the garden or grow them separately and mix them in the salad bowl.

That's mesclun. You can make your own mesclun mixes by buying seeds of your favorite greens (lettuces, chicories, cresses, arugula, chervil, and others) and mixing them together. Or you can buy special mixes already prepared as either "mild" or "piquant"—the latter containing more of the chicories and other stronger-flavored herbs and greens. A prepared mesclun mix is not a bad idea for new gardeners who are not familiar with the growing habits of all the greens they'd like to mix. It is vital that the greens you select for your *mesclun* not only taste good together in a salad but grow together well in an intensively planted bed. And remember, too, that the sky's the limit as far as combinations are concerned—as long as you're conscious of the cultural needs of the plants.

In any case, sow your mixture in a wide bed either broadcast or in shallow drills (¼ inch deep), about 4 to 6 inches apart in the bed. The Cook's Garden catalog advises planting 6 to 8 feet of bed per week for a steady supply of luscious greens.

Mesclun is harvested by the cut-and-come-again method when plants are very young, about 2 to 3 inches tall. You can expect several cuttings from a single patch before the greens turn too bitter.

Mesclun Possibilities

Mild mixes generally include mostly lettuces with a chicory or two. French mescluns combine romaine and butterhead lettuces, arugula, chicory, and chervil. Traditional *misticanza* mixes are stronger and usually blend four kinds of lettuce and five chicories, for the Italians are fond of their radicchio. But the idea is to blend flavors and textures and colors without destroying the integrity of any single one.

The following list offers plant combinations of different colors and flavors. They are not meant to be exhaustive, and you can certainly add to them, either in the garden or in the salad bowl.

PLANTS FOR COLOR

Red lettuces, red chicories, red cabbage, flowering mustards, ornamental kales, red peppers, tomatoes, edible flowers (nasturtiums, borages, pansies, etc.)

PLANTS FOR STRONG FLAVOR

Chicories, mustards, cresses, spinach, chard, cilantro, shungiku, sorrel, arugula, dandelion, bunching onions, garlic, chives, endive

PLANTS FOR MILD FLAVOR

Lettuces, mâche, parsley, chives, Mizuna (Japanese mustard), orach, purslane, chard, ornamental kale, Belgian endive, claytonia, amaranth spinach, celtuce

PLANTS FOR CRUNCH

Carrots, celery, celtuce, radishes, sweet fennel, cucumbers, broccoli, cauliflower, Belgian endive, peppers

Here are a few other salad greens to try in your mesclun mix. My experience with them is limited, except to say that they are easy to grow and they introduce interesting flavors to the salad bowl.

Spinach dock has a lemony flavor similar to sorrel (see page 135).

Good King Henry has a spinachlike flavor and both stems and leaves are excellent in salads.

Ice plant, known also as fig marigold, generally appears in the annual flower border. But the salty-tasting leaves provide interesting flavor in salads.

Some gardeners, including myself, spend years trying to get rid of **Purslane,** but the French cultivate a fleshier, somewhat more citrus-flavored version which is delightful in salads.

I first learned about **claytonia** (also called miner's lettuce) as a seedling crop from Joy Larkcom and ordered it from the Cook's Garden catalog. It is mild-flavored and attractive in the salad bowl.

I ordered **curled mallow** seeds for the first time a couple of years ago from Pinetree Garden Seeds. Plants grow very tall, and the leaves are nice in salads, if a little bland.

*Salad Greens
and Herbs*

SALAD HERBS

The fourteen herbs which are discussed in this section have a range of uses. You can use them fresh—in salads, herbal vinegars (see page 130), or salad dressings. Many can also be dried and used in dressings and about a million other recipes. Our focus here, of course, is using herbs in salad.

Because most herbs have strong, distinctive flavors, it is generally considered wise to use them sparingly in salads to avoid overpowering the blander and less aromatic ingredients on the plate. If you're unfamiliar with the use of fresh salad herbs, experiment; you'll soon discover what you like and what you don't. For example, if the leaves are large or particularly powerful, such as those of chives and traditional basil varieties, I like to chop them and add the quantity I find appropriate to my taste. When leaves are small, on the other hand, as with thyme, miniature basil, and sweet marjoram, I like to use them whole.

There's no reason why you couldn't grow almost all of the herbs on our list this year—even if your garden is tiny—for most are well suited to container cultivation. You may not get lavish harvests, but you'll have more than enough herbs for your salads.

Some of these herbs are annuals, which means they live and die in a single season. Others are biennials, meaning they live for two years, growing leaves and good strong roots the first year and setting seed the second year. A small number of our group are perennials, returning year after year if given the proper attention.

Naturally, if you have the space, a separate herb garden can be an inspiring project. Lacking the ambition to design a special herb garden, you could easily integrate the annual and biennial herbs with your salad vegetables and establish a small separate bed for your perennials. If your garden plan changes next year, don't worry; perennial herbs are easily moved.

GARDEN CRESS

The Salad Lover's
GARDEN

BASIL

Basil, an annual also called sweet basil, is one of the easiest and most satisfying to grow of all the herbs. Its fragrance is enchanting to me, though in *Culpeper's Complete Herbal and English Physician* of 1652, the French physician Hilarius "affirms upon his own knowledge that, an acquaintance of his, by common smelling of it, had a scorpion bred in his brain."

You can start basil indoors to get a jump on the season, but I've always had perfectly good luck direct-seeding in the garden when the soil has thoroughly warmed. Though mature plants will want about 12 to 18 inches around themselves, sow seeds 1 inch apart in shallow drills and thin the bed when the seedlings have their first true leaves. At this stage, they're excellent in salads. Napoletano, Lemon basil, Lettuce Leaf basil, Spicy Globe, and Purple Ruffles are some of the many types you can try. Basil will also grow quite nicely in a south-facing windowsill pot all year long.

Pinch back tops when plants are 5 to 6 inches tall to promote bushy growth. Pinch back flower shoots. Harvest individual leaves or shoots as needed.

BASIL AT A GLANCE

BASIL

SOW INDOORS OR UNDER GLASS: 6 to 8 weeks before last frost.

GERMINATION: 7 to 10 days.

DIRECT-SEED OUTDOORS: When soil is thoroughly warm.

PLANT OUT: After all danger of frost.

SEED DEPTH: ¼ inch.

DISTANCE BETWEEN PLANTS: 12 to 18 inches.

SOIL: Average, well drained; pH 6.0 to 7.0.

SUNLIGHT: Full sun.

WATER: Steady supply.

FEEDING: Unnecessary.

*Salad Greens
and Herbs*

BORAGE

I, Borage, bring alwaies courage.

—*Gerard's Herball*

Known as the herb of gladness for its ability (according to a seventeenth-century English herbal) to "expel pensiveness and melancholy . . . ," this tall and gorgeous annual plant (it will reach heights of 3 to 4 feet) offers salad lovers not only its sweet cucumber-flavored leaves, but the bluest of blue star-shaped edible flowers. Pick leaves young, for they develop an unpleasant fuzz to them when they get older, and chop them into salads. Stems can also be stripped and chopped into the dish.

Pick flowers just before they open.

BORAGE

BORAGE AT A GLANCE

SOW INDOORS OR UNDER GLASS: Not an indoor starter.

GERMINATION: 7 to 10 days.

DIRECT-SEED OUTDOORS: In early spring and again in midsummer for a second crop.

SEED DEPTH: 1¼ inches.

DISTANCE BETWEEN PLANTS: 18 inches.

SOIL: Average soil is fine, but plants will also thrive in moist, rich soil.

SUNLIGHT: Full sun.

WATER: Sparingly; usually necessary only during dry spells.

FEEDING: Not necessary.

CHERVIL

Chervil is a hardy biennial often grown as an annual.

Given chervil's tendency to go to seed when hot weather arrives, the best way to keep yourself in good supply of this genial parsley-anise flavored herb is to sow a fresh crop every three weeks from early spring through late summer. Alternatively, be on guard for flower stalks and clip them off as soon as you see them. Let a few bolt toward the end of the season and store them for next year's stash of seeds.

Chervil leaves can be tossed into salads in spriglets, or you can chop them first, as you would parsley. Sprigs of the lacy flowers make a delicate garnish. Chervil is also wonderful in omelets, soups, and sauces. Chervil, chives, tarragon, and marjoram form the traditional French *fines herbes* mixture. Try this combination to flavor an herbal vinegar.

Pick chervil leaves just before flower buds open.

CHERVIL AT A GLANCE

CHERVIL

SOW INDOORS OR UNDER GLASS: Not a good indoor starter.

GERMINATION: 7 to 14 days.

DIRECT-SEED OUTDOORS: 3 weeks before last frost, and again in late summer for overwintering in areas with mild winters.

SEED DEPTH: ¼ inch.

DISTANCE BETWEEN PLANTS: 8 inches.

SOIL: Rich, well drained.

SUNLIGHT: Full sun.

WATER: Sparingly and only when soil becomes dry.

FEEDING: Not necessary.

*Salad Greens
and Herbs*

CHIVES

No garden should be without this mild-flavored perennial member of the onion family. Chives can be grown from seed indoors, direct-seeded in the garden early in spring, or started from nursery-bought plants. Once you've got a clump of chives, you'll never be without them again. The only attention they need the first season is weeding and watering. Once established, they're as hardy as any edible plant anywhere.

Chive clumps should be divided every few years. Use a sharp spade to make the divisions, each of which can start another clump. Your chiveless friends will appreciate these divisions when you come bearing them as gifts. Also be on the lookout for seeds of garlic or Chinese chives, which produce flat, garlic-flavored leaves and starry white flowers.

Chop chives into salads in place of scallions, and for a special treat, steep the lovely pink flowers in white distilled vinegar. A week later, the vinegar will be bright pink and ready for display in a sunny window—and then, of course, for use in salad dressings.

Use sharp scissors to harvest leaves as needed. Discard the flower stems, as they're not tender or particularly tasty.

CHIVES

The Salad Lover's
GARDEN

CHIVES AT A GLANCE

SOW INDOORS OR UNDER GLASS: In early spring.

GERMINATION: 7 to 14 days.

DIRECT-SEED OUTDOORS: 3 weeks before last frost.

PLANT OUT: Set out clumps of seedlings or root divisions a week or two before last frost.

SEED DEPTH: ¼ inch.

DISTANCE BETWEEN PLANTS: 12 inches.

SOIL: Rich, moist soil is ideal, but average soil will do.

SUNLIGHT: Full sun, but they will also do well in partial shade.

WATER: Only during dry spells.

FEEDING: Apply manure or compost annually, especially when dividing roots.

CILANTRO

Known also as Chinese parsley for its leaves and coriander for its seeds, cilantro (*seel-ON-tro*) is a strong-flavored annual which is used primarily in Mexican and Asian cooked dishes. But this parsley look-alike may also be chopped and added very frugally to fresh salads when the leaves are young.

Sow in wide beds, either broadcast or in shallow drills. Like chervil, cilantro is likely to bolt in warm weather, at which time the quality of the plant goes downhill fast; so plan on succession crops if you want a reliable stock. Use slow-bolting varieties when you can find them. Plants freely self-sow, so be vigilant about removing the seeds before they fall.

Plants can be cut back several times before going to seed; harvest the seeds for coriander when they've turned brown. Clip the stems and hang them upside down in a paper bag until the seeds are fully dried, then shake the seeds into the bag.

CILANTRO

CILANTRO AT A GLANCE

SOW INDOORS OR UNDER GLASS: Not a good indoor starter.

GERMINATION: 7 to 14 days.

DIRECT-SEED OUTDOORS: 3 weeks before last frost, and every few weeks thereafter for a continuous supply.

SEED DEPTH: ¼ inch.

DISTANCE BETWEEN PLANTS: 6 to 8 inches.

SOIL: Average, but well drained.

SUNLIGHT: Full sun.

WATER: Steady, moderate supply.

FEEDING: Unnecessary.

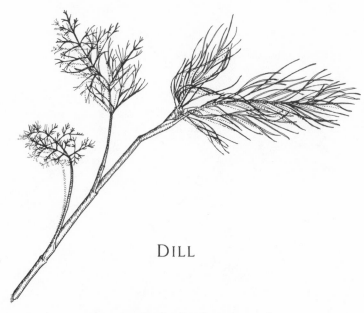

DILL

Mercury hath the dominion of
this plant, and therefore to be sure it
strengthens the brain. It stayeth the
hiccough, being boiled in wine, and
but smelled into, being
tied in a cloth.

—*Culpeper's Complete Herbal and English Physician*

Where would I be without dill? I love it; I can't get enough of it. In salads of all kinds, for pickles, for soups and vegetable dishes, for dips. I have never tried eating dill roots, but all other parts of this annual plant are edible—leaves, stems, and seeds, the last growing aloft in great green sprays.

Dill is easy to grow; you'll find that wide-row growing offers efficiency of scale. For beginners, however, two cautions. First, when you sow the seeds, don't cover them with soil; instead firm the seed in place with a flat board or your hand. Second, don't lose patience while waiting for dill seedlings to germinate—they can take up to a

127

Salad Greens
and Herbs

month. Try a few succession plantings if you love dill. Otherwise, follow the directions that follow and you'll do fine.

When plants are 4 to 5 inches tall, you can start cutting the feathery fronds—about a month after germination.

Dill at a Glance

SOW INDOORS OR UNDER GLASS: 6 weeks before last frost.

GERMINATION: 21 to 28 days.

DIRECT-SEED OUTDOORS: 3 weeks before last frost.

PLANT OUT: When threat of frost is past.

SEED DEPTH: Press seeds lightly into soil; they require light to germinate.

DISTANCE BETWEEN PLANTS: 8 to 12 inches.

SOIL: Rich, well drained.

SUNLIGHT: Full sun.

WATER: Steady supply.

FEEDING: Unnecessary if soil is fairly rich.

OREGANO

Indeed sir, she was the
sweet marjoram of the sallet, or
rather the herb of grace.

—*All's Well That Ends Well*

OREGANO

Oregano (*Origanum vulgare*), a hardy perennial, produces small, spicy-flavored leaves which are excellent in salads and, when dried, are a staple ingredient in what is commonly referred to as "Italian" dressing. It is easy to grow, either from seeds or from cuttings. Give oregano its own spot in the perennial bed and keep it well trimmed or it will spread all over creation. Sweet marjoram, (*O. majorana*), a more delicately flavored and aromatic annual cousin of oregano's, will also spread out about 2 feet itself, but once the season is over, it's over.

New plantings of oregano or sweet marjoram can be made by taking cuttings from the parent plant, so your trimmings need not be wasted, if that's something you'd worry about. Where winters are mild, oregano will remain green and pickable all year. Otherwise, cuttings can be transferred to pots on the sill of a south-facing window and grown successfully indoors year-round.

Harvesting can begin as soon as leaves appear. Harvest before plants flower if you want to dry the leaves.

HERBAL VINEGARS

What pleasure there is in the midwinter uncorking of a bottle of homemade herbal vinegar! It recalls in a whiff all the fragrant essence of the summer herb garden.

Herbal vinegars add a gourmet touch to all your salads, are surprisingly easy to make, and—lined up in glass bottles on a sunny windowsill (see the Williams-Sonoma catalog for their selection of Spanish glass bottles)—are quite a beautiful addition to the salad lover's kitchen.

The vinegars best for herbal flavoring are those that absorb flavors, such as white wine, champagne, apple cider, and Japanese rice wine vinegars. Some herbalists prefer plain white distilled vinegar.

Herbs that are especially flavorful in vinegars include basil, borage, chives, dill, fennel, garlic, horseradish, marjoram, oregano, tarragon, thyme, and winter savory with chili peppers. Use one cup of fresh herbs to one pint of vinegar.

To make herbal vinegar, lightly bruise the herbs to release their flavor, and press them into bottles. Gently warm vinegar over a low flame and pour into the bottles with the help of a small funnel. Place the bottles on a windowsill or some other place where they'll receive light. Let the mixture steep for ten to fourteen days, shaking the bottles once a day.

At the end of the steeping period, test for taste. For stronger flavor, strain out the herbs with cheesecloth, a sieve, or even a paper coffee filter, add a fresh batch of herbs, and steep for another week or so.

If the vinegar will be used within a few months' time, then standard tight lids will suffice for storage. But if you think these vinegars might linger for half a year or longer, consider sealing them with a cork and wax. Label and date each bottle with an indelible marker.

OREGANO AT A GLANCE

SOW INDOORS OR UNDER GLASS: Early spring.

GERMINATION: 10 to 14 days.

DIRECT-SEED OUTDOORS: 3 weeks before last frost.

PLANT OUT: Seedlings or root divisions of oregano, 2 to 3 weeks before last frost; after frost for sweet marjoram.

SEED DEPTH: ¼ inch.

DISTANCE BETWEEN PLANTS: 12 inches, and let them run together.

SOIL: Light, well drained.

SUNLIGHT: Full sun.

WATER: Only during dry spells.

FEEDING: Apply manure or compost annually when dividing roots.

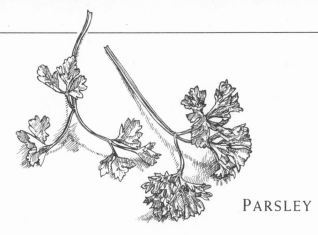

PARSLEY

Lamentably, raw parsley in America is used largely as a garnish. That's not the case at my house, where we throw handfuls of it together with wild chicory, dandelion greens, chervil, and a few leaves of red romaine and serve the salad under a light oil and lemon dressing for an end-of-meal delight.

Of the two principal types of parsley available, I much prefer the flat-leaf variety over the curly because it is, to my taste at least, the more tender and more flavorful. Parsley shares one annoying trait with that most pleasant of garden herbs, dill, and that is its infuriating reluctance to germinate quickly. You can try soaking the seed overnight before planting but it may not hasten germination by more than a couple of days. Once seeds germinate, if you keep the soil moist, you should have no trouble bringing in an excellent crop.

One final note. Because parsley is a biennial, it will survive even severe winters and put on new growth in the spring. In my experience, however, only the very first of this new growth comes even close to the superior flavor of first-season parsley, so I've abandoned the practice of letting it overwinter and start a fresh crop each spring.

FLAT-LEAF PARSLEY

You can begin your harvest as soon as there are a few leaves to pinch, though it is best to wait until you can cut a few stems to within an inch of the soil. If you let parsley overwinter, harvest leaves the following year before plants flower.

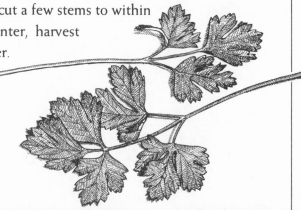

PARSLEY AT A GLANCE

SOW INDOORS OR UNDER GLASS: 6 to 8 weeks before last frost.

GERMINATION: 14 to 21 days.

DIRECT-SEED OUTDOORS: 2 weeks before last frost; in mild climates, direct-sow in the fall.

PLANT OUT: 2 weeks before last frost.

SEED DEPTH: ¼ inch.

DISTANCE BETWEEN PLANTS: 6 to 10 inches.

SOIL: Rich, moist, well drained.

SUNLIGHT: Full sun is best, but it will do well in partial shade too.

WATER: Steady supply; don't let soil dry out.

FEEDING: Topdress with manure or compost when plants are 6 inches tall.

SAGE

Although the perennial sage is available in many varieties and colors, most are a bit too pungent for salads—as far as I'm concerned—and are best left for cooked dishes, marinades, and salad vinegars (e.g., a sprig of golden sage steeped in wine or sherry vinegar).

One exception is pineapple sage, which is grown as an annual everywhere north of the tropics. This delightful herb offers a charming spice and pineapple flavor when coarsely chopped into salads. And its red flowers can also be added to the salad bowl with wonderful effect.

Being a broadleaf type, pineapple sage never sets seed (or hardly ever does) and must be grown from cuttings. Because sage naturally propagates itself by layering (the tips of the stems bend over and root in the soil), you can take tip cuttings from parent plants or stem cuttings with a heel to start new plants.

Pinch a few leaves when you need them. For larger harvests, cut in midsummer before plants flower and again in late summer.

SAGE AT A GLANCE

SOW INDOORS OR UNDER GLASS: Only narrow-leaved varieties are started from seed.

PLANT OUT: 3 weeks before last frost.

DISTANCE BETWEEN PLANTS: 12 inches.

SOIL: Light, well-drained soil ideal; pH 6.0 to 7.0.

SUNLIGHT: Full sun.

WATER: Keep seedbeds moist; thereafter, water only during dry spells.

FEEDING: Unnecessary.

SAGE

Salad Greens
and Herbs

SALAD BURNET

Not to be confused with burnet saxifrage (known also as lesser burnet), which is grown for the medicinal qualities of its root, salad burnet forms pleasant little mounds of serrated, cucumber-flavored leaves which lend an almost effervescent quality to any salad.

I got my first root divisions from a friend (the plant is perennial) and have propagated new plants over the years from that original stock. However, salad burnet is just as easily started outdoors from seed. The soil must be near neutral, so it wouldn't hurt to lime your bed a bit before planting. Cover the seed only barely with sifted peat moss or compost. Be sparing with the water, as salad burnet prefers soil on the dry side. As with other herbs, the more vigilant you are about removing flower stems from salad burnet, the more concentrated will be the flavor of its leaves.

Begin harvesting when leaves are ⅓ inch long.

SALAD BURNET

SALAD BURNET AT A GLANCE

SOW INDOORS OR UNDER GLASS: Not a good indoor starter.

GERMINATION: 10 days.

DIRECT-SEED OUTDOORS: Sow seed or set out root divisions in midspring.

SEED DEPTH: ⅛ inch.

DISTANCE BETWEEN PLANTS: 12 inches.

SOIL: Average soil; pH 6.5 to 7.0.

SUNLIGHT: Full sun.

WATER: Sparingly.

FEEDING: Dig in manure or compost annually.

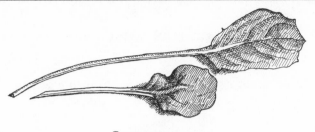

SORREL

Sorrel is one of those special salad herbs that hardly anyone uses—least of all fresh in salads. Seed catalogs generally offer French (or "true" French) sorrel, a smaller-leaved type, grown widely for use in sorrel soup. Both French and garden sorrel are perennials. I've grown both types and find their tangy, citrusy flavor equally satisfying, especially in the first salads of spring when wild dandelion, chicory, and chives are abundant. As any sorrel lover will warn you, a few of the lemon-flavored leaves go a long way. However much you may enjoy them, be stingy or they'll overpower the salad.

Start seeds indoors or out in early spring. Plants spaced 4 inches apart will produce a steady supply of young leaves for salads. Spaced at 10 inches, sorrel will produce bushy plants for heavier harvests. Sorel can be harvested right through the hard frosts of autumn, and it will, along with chives, make an early showing in spring.

After a few years, the plants begin to weaken and should be divided to start new plants. Or you can take the lazy way out and let a few flower stalks go to seed (only a few, mind you, or sorrel will take over the garden), and the plants will reliably self-sow. Transplant the new seedlings elsewhere and you're in business.

First-year harvests can be made in midsummer. Strip off outside leaves to encourage production.

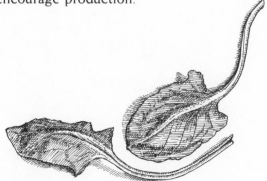

*Salad Greens
and Herbs*

SORREL AT A GLANCE

SOW INDOORS OR UNDER GLASS: 3 to 4 weeks before setting out.

GERMINATION: 14 days.

DIRECT-SEED OUTDOORS: 3 weeks before last frost.

PLANT OUT: 3 weeks before last frost.

SEED DEPTH: ¼ inch.

DISTANCE BETWEEN PLANTS: 4 inches for just young leaves; 10 inches for larger plants.

SOIL: Rich, well drained, though sorrel will produce in average soil.

SUNLIGHT: Full sun to light shade.

WATER: Keep soil moist but not muddy.

FEEDING: Unnecessary.

SWEET FENNEL

Sweet fennel or Florence fennel is no newcomer to my garden, though it took me some years to catch on to it as a salad ingredient. Since then I've learned to prize its succulent, anise-scented crunch above celery.

Sweet fennel is a perennial grown as an annual. Quite remarkable in its appearance, it grows large sprays of dill-like leaves on stems whose bases eventually swell, one atop another, into a bulb the size of a baseball that sits just above the soil surface. Simply slice the thickened leaf bases into strips and add them to salads. The leaves can be used like those of regular fennel as a flavoring for cooking fish, and the flowers eventually produce seeds (if you let them) which are refreshing when chewed. The English long believed that the leaves, seeds, and bulbs steeped in drink or a broth would "make people lean that are too fat." Not a bad reason to try it, eh?

137

*Salad Greens
and Herbs*

Start plants under cover and transplant to the garden when they've developed a few of their feathery leaves, or sow in a cold frame about three weeks before the last frost and thin plants to stand 12 inches apart. The soil should be rich to begin with, though the bulbs will appreciate a topdressing of compost as they take on bulk. Hill up the thickened stems with soil a week or so before harvest, and the naturally strong licorice flavor will be attenuated.

Harvest leaves when you can; cut the bulb just above the soil when it is 3 to 4 inches in diameter. If you're lucky, you may get modest regrowth.

SWEET FENNEL AT A GLANCE

SOW INDOORS OR UNDER GLASS: 5 weeks before setting out.

GERMINATION: 10 to 14 days.

DIRECT-SEED OUTDOORS: Best seeded in flats or shaded cold frame, about 3 weeks before the last frost.

PLANT OUT: When seedlings have their first set of true leaves.

SEED DEPTH: ¼ inch.

DISTANCE BETWEEN PLANTS: 12 inches.

SOIL: Rich, well drained.

SUNLIGHT: Full sun.

WATER: Keep watered during dry spells.

FEEDING: Topdress with aged manure or compost when bulb starts to thicken.

The Salad Lover's
GARDEN

Lettuce (Salad Bowl), Cook's Garden, Londonderry, Vt.

Lettuce (Sierra), Cook's Garden, Londonderry, Vt.

Lettuce (Reine des Glaces), Cook's Garden, Londonderry, Vt.

Tomatoes, Sam Bittman's garden, Cheshire, Mass.

Kale (Nerodi Toscana), Cook's Garden, Londonderry, Vt.

Lettuce (Salad Bowl/LaRosa), Cook's Garden, Londonderry, Vt.

Fire bean, Cook's Garden, Londonderry, Vt.

Herb garden, Blantyre Hotel, Lenox, Mass.

Herb garden, Blantyre Hotel, Lenox, Mass.

Herb shop and edible flower garden,
Meadowsweet Herb Farm, Shrewsbury, Vt.

Flowering cabbage, dwarf parsley, painted sage,
and dwarf curry, Meadowsweet Herb Farm, Shrewsbury, Vt.

Salad herb garden, Meadowsweet Herb Farm, Shrewsbury, Vt.

Marigolds and nasturtiums, Meadowsweet Herb Farm, Shrewsbury, Vt.

Herb garden, Mission House, Stockbridge, Mass.

TARRAGON

When I first started gardening and someone told me I could actually *grow* tarragon, I was enchanted. I don't know where I thought it came from, or that I had ever wondered, frankly, but this I can tell you: When my lips uttered "tarragon" my mind conjured Arabian spice caravans. I can't fathom why, as it is best known as an ingredient in French dishes. Nevertheless, the idea of raising it was thrilling.

FRENCH TARRAGON

And it was easier to grow than I could have imagined. What I learned was that you can't start true French tarragon from seed, since it rarely if ever *sets* seed. Rather, you start it from cuttings or root divisions taken from someone else's plant, or set out young plants from a nursery or garden center. Russian tarragon, which is coarser and less flavorful than French tarragon, *can* be started from seed.

In either case, set plants about 18 to 24 inches apart and keep well watered until they are well established. Once the plants are 6 inches high, you can make your first light harvest of a stem here and there. Although it's a perennial, French tarragon should be renewed every few years from cuttings in order to maintain peak flavor. And if your perennial herb patch is exposed to harsh winters, you might consider mulching your tarragon with straw or pine boughs before the ground freezes hard.

In the salad bowl, tarragon should be used a few leaves at a time, or its somewhat aniselike flavor may overpower the entire dish. Sprigs of tarragon can be steeped in wine vinegar for an excellent homemade vinegar.

Harvest first-year plants moderately; leaves of established plants can be picked at will, or cut heavily for drying three times during the growing season.

RUSSIAN TARRAGON

TARRAGON AT A GLANCE

SOW INDOORS OR UNDER GLASS: Russian tarragon, 4 weeks before last frost.

GERMINATION: 20 to 25 days.

DIRECT-SEED OUTDOORS: Russian tarragon, in midspring.

PLANT OUT: Set out plants, cuttings, or root divisions of French tarragon in late spring.

SEED DEPTH: ¼ inch.

DISTANCE BETWEEN PLANTS: 18 to 24 inches.

SOIL: Rich, well drained.

SUNLIGHT: Full sun or light shade.

WATER: Steady supply.

FEEDING: Topdress with compost in early spring and late summer.

THYME

There are scores of perennial thymes available to gardeners, but the variety I like best for salads is lemon thyme. It has a hint of the same tangy bittersweetness of other culinary thymes, but with a touch of lemon. Chop the small leaves fine or add them whole to any salad for a little something extra. Lemon thyme also makes a great vinegar and when dried is a welcome addition to any salad dressing.

You can start thyme indoors, but if you lack the growing facilities, it will do equally well from root divisions you can buy at any good nursery. Give each plant a wide berth, as thyme tends to meander. Cut back plants before winter and again in spring to encourage growth. Renew your planting each year from cuttings or by root division.

Harvest once the first year, just as blossoms open. In subsequent years, make two major harvests. Of course, you can pick sprigs anytime.

THYME AT A GLANCE

SOW INDOORS OR UNDER GLASS: 8 weeks before last frost.

GERMINATION: 21 to 30 days.

DIRECT-SEED OUTDOORS: 3 weeks before last frost.

PLANT OUT: 3 weeks before last frost.

SEED DEPTH: ¼ inch.

DISTANCE BETWEEN PLANTS: 10 inches.

SOIL: Light, well drained.

SUNLIGHT: Full sun.

WATER: Only during dry spells.

FEEDING: Unnecessary.

THYME

Salad Greens and Herbs

Salad Oils

When the Old Testament psalmist wrote about "oil to make his face to shine," he was no doubt referring to the glow of health promoted by the judicious use of good olive oil, not to mention the simple enjoyment of its rich golden-green taste.

Today, though, the difficulty of sorting out the significance of safflowers, monounsaturates, cholesterol levels, cold-pressing, and extra virgin seems like a high price to pay for greasing a few greens. But choosing good oils for your salad dressings will be well worth the effort. For clarity's sake, here's a look at the vocabulary of taste, quality, and healthfulness of current salad oils.

Oil Flavor Guide

Avocado oil is rich and sweet, and it enhances bitter greens such as radicchio, dandelion, and endive.

Olive oil, like wine, is affected by the soil where the fruit is grown. Italian olive oil has a light, nutty flavor; Spanish oil is stronger. Greek olive oil is thicker in texture, and French Provençal has a fruity taste. For salads, the best virgin oil is recommended.

Soybean oil is bland and light for salad dressing mixes. Many refined oils are made from soybeans.

Sunflower oil is delicate, gentle, and good for light salad dressings, for mild greens such as Bibb, butterhead, or iceberg lettuce.

Safflower oil is light and bland, providing a medium for flavors more pronounced than its own.

A relative newcomer to the oil selection is canola oil, which is made from rapeseed and produced in Canada. It has a light texture and taste.

Glossary of Oil Terms

Cold-pressed oils offer the best flavor. The fruit or seed hasn't been heated above 110°F to extract the oil.

"Expeller-pressed oils" is a term sometimes seen on labels in health-food stores. These oils have been extracted without the use of hexane, a petroleum solvent and carcinogen, traces of which may remain after the process.

Refining, or removing impurities, diminishes some of the oil's flavor but gives it a longer shelf life.

Antioxidants such as BHA and BHT increase shelf life and inhibit damaging oxidation. Light and heat oxidize oils, causing them to produce substances which can irritate inner artery walls, where fatty deposits can collect.

Extra virgin and superfine virgin oil are obtained from the first light pressing of handpicked olives, without heating. Fine virgin and virgin oils are also cold-pressed, but they are not as light in color or flavor. "Pure" olive oil—or simply "olive oil"—is extracted from the residue of these virgin pressings using heat and chemical solvents.

Oil Health Notes

Health-conscious dieters concerned about preventing heart disease by controlling cholesterol levels look to vegetable oils for good taste and low fat content. But there's more to it than that: The health benefits of various oils are based on their proportions of saturated fats, polyunsaturates, and monounsaturates.

Saturated fats lead to overproduction of cholesterol and increase low-density lipoproteins, which deposit cholesterol in arteries. Some oils contain no cholesterol but are highly saturated. Intake of saturated fats is a major factor in heart disease.

Polyunsaturated oils, such as corn and soybean oils, are the usual health standbys of the supermarket, but the jury is still out on the extent of their benefits. These oils are often hydrogenated for better consistency and longer shelf life, which makes them more difficult for the body to break down.

Monounsaturated fats lower the amount of low-density lipoproteins in the bloodstream and increase high-density lipoproteins, which return excess fats and cholesterol to the liver for recycling (instead of dumping them in the arteries). "Mono" oils, such as olive, peanut, avocado, and canola oils, seem to be the heroes in reducing incidence of heart disease, and they may also help hold down blood pressure.

Here's a rating of oils in terms of their proportions of monounsaturates (m), polyunsaturates (p), and saturates (s):

Avocado	M: 70%	P: 16%	S: 14%
Canola	M: 62%	P: 32%	S: 6%
Olive	M: 73%	P: 11%	S: 16%
Soybean	M: 24%	P: 62%	S: 15%
Sunflower	M: 19%	P: 70%	S: 12%
Safflower	M: 13%	P: 77%	S: 10%

Oil should be stored in a cool, dark place. Unrefined oils can be stored for up to a year, refined oils for two years. It's a good idea to decant a small amount for daily kitchen or table use and keep the rest in a tightly capped bottle.

You can use flavored oils and infusions to add interest to salad dressings. To make flavored oil, you can steep garlic, dried chili peppers, or rosemary in olive oil. When garlic is steeped in oil, an acidifying agent such as citrus zest or chili peppers must be added to prevent harmful bacteria from forming. As an additional precaution, the U.S. Food and Drug Administration recommends refrigerating all flavored oils. Use a good-quality olive oil and refrigerate for a few weeks before using to allow flavors to permeate the oil.

EDIBLE FLOWERS

Highlights of color not only in your garden but also in your salads, edible flowers add new dimensions of taste, texture, and appearance. As borders in or around your garden, in bright beds of their own, or even as trailing vines amid your other crops, they provide edible landscaping, too.

Flowers for eating have a noble heritage; they were a delicacy enjoyed by Roman patricians, Charlemagne's courtiers, and Victorian households. So that you can carry on the tradition, here's a selection of edible flowers recommended for salads.

- *Bean blossoms:* Besides juicy runner beans, the variety Painted Lady produces an abundance of great-tasting white and coral blossoms with a crisp texture and sweet beany flavor. The blossoms are delicious in salads, and the vines look pretty growing over fences or arches. Available from Shepherd's.

- *Borage:* The blue, star-shaped flowers of this tall and hardy annual herb add a cool cucumber taste to your salads. Some flower eaters prefer to remove the hairy sepals from the blossoms. The borage plant likes full sun and will grow to be 3 or 4 feet tall. Another bonus of these blue flowers is their attraction for bees. The blossoms can also be candied or frozen in ice cubes to flavor drinks. Available from a variety of sources.

- *Calendula:* The variety Kablouna is recommended; it's easy to grow in cool summer areas, and it produces orange, gold, and yellow blossoms from early summer to frost. The delicately flavored petals add bright color and a subtle peppery taste to summer salads. Calendula is another full-sun plant, and it will grow to 1½ feet tall. Available from Cook's Garden, Shepherd's.

- *Chives:* The purple-pink flowers of chives have a delicate onion flavor; the blooms are most tender when the buds first open. The plant is easy to grow and is an attractive addition to any garden, and the blossoms add taste, color, and texture to salad creations. Available from a variety of sources.

- *Johnny-jump-ups:* These sprightly little flowers have a mild wintergreen taste for a pleasant salad addition. A border or containerful of the purple and yellow blooms—they look like miniature pansies—is especially nice near the kitchen. Available from a variety of sources.

- *Marigold:* The old-fashioned version of this popular flower adds a citrusy tang to green salads. The variety Lemon Gem grows in neat mounds with masses of single half-inch yellow blossoms. Foliage and flowers have a lemon scent. Tangerine Gem is similar, with an orange bloom. Mix the blossoms in a border or in a salad for effect. Available from Shepherd's.

- *Nasturtiums:* For their peppery watercress flavor and bright colors for salad accents, nasturtiums are favorite edible flowers. The variety Whirlybird is recommended for a sweet but mildly spicy taste, like watercress with a drop of honey. This variety also boasts 2 ½-inch double blooms on dwarf plants, with a variety of unusual hues such as cream, salmon, and mahogany. The blooms have no spur, so they're easy to clean for eating. Nasturtiums grow well in poor soil and will bloom until hard frost. Baskets or beds in sun or light shade areas will display beautiful 6-to-8-inch mounds of blooms. Available from Cook's Garden, Shepherd's. Also from Shepherd's is the new variety Empress of India, with vermilion, single-spur red blossoms growing in cascading clumps.

- *Sage flowers:* Clary sage boasts long spikes of mauve and pink flowers from midsummer to fall. Sprinkled on salads, they give color and fragrance.

The best time to pick flowers for your salad is when they are at their freshest, as early in the day as they are dry. Cut and handle (and wash, if necessary) gently, so they won't be bruised. They will keep for the day in a closed bag in the refrigerator. Add small whole flowers or petals to the salad just before serving, and after adding the dressing.

Please note: some flowers are poisonous, some extremely so. For consumption, be sure to use only the blossoms you know are safe.

Grilled Chicory Salad

FROM ANGELS RESTAURANT, PROVIDENCE, R.I.
JAIME D'OLIVEIRA, CHEF

2 heads Belgian endive

2 heads radicchio

2 heads frisée or 1 large head chicory

½ cup extra virgin olive oil

3 tablespoons sherry wine vinegar

½ teaspoon salt

freshly ground black pepper to taste

½ cup raw pistachio nuts, shelled and chopped

Prepare grill. Light a charcoal fire and allow 35 to 40 minutes for the grill to reach the right temperature. Coals should be glowing red hot under a light gray ash.

To make the dressing, whisk together the oil and vinegar with approximately ½ teaspoon salt and freshly ground black pepper to taste.

Slice radicchio and Belgian endive in half vertically. If using frisée, divide similarly; if using chicory, divide the head into four equal parts. Brush with olive oil. Place endive on hot grill. After 2 minutes, place radicchio on the grill. After 2 more minutes, place frisée or chicory on the grill. This last green will cook quite quickly. Turn the greens as necessary for even grilling. Greens should retain some of their original texture.

Arrange one of each type of chicory attractively on each plate. Brush with the dressing and then drizzle more dressing around the salad on the plate. Sprinkle with pistachio nuts and garnish with lemon wedges.

Serves 4.

The Salad Lover's
GARDEN

Savory Salad of Arugula, Hazelnuts, and Blue Castello Timbale

FROM CHATEAU SOUVERAIN, GEYSERVILLE, CALIF.
GARY DANKO, CHEF

4 bunches arugula, smallish and tender leaves

HAZELNUT DRESSING

4 teaspoons hazelnut oil

½ teaspoon heavy cream

¼ teaspoon each Dijon mustard and lemon juice

salt and pepper to taste

2 tablespoons hazelnuts, toasted, peeled, and chopped

Whisk together all ingredients except for hazelnuts.

TIMBALE

4 ounces Blue Castello

2 tablespoons unsalted butter, soft

4 ounces cream cheese

1 clove garlic

3 large eggs

3 tablespoons heavy cream

salt and pepper to taste

1 tablespoon chopped chives

Combine all ingredients except chives in a food processor. Blend until smooth. Strain and add chives. (This may be done ahead.) Divide mixture between four 4-ounce timbale molds that have been well buttered. Bake in a water bath for 20 to 25 minutes.

Unmold onto individual plates and accompany with small salad tossed with hazelnut dressing. Sprinkle with hazelnuts and serve.

Serves 4. (Wine suggestion: Chateau Souverain Zinfandel, Dry Creek Valley.)

147

Salad Greens
and Herbs

Savory Lettuce, Goat Cheese, and Petite Green Bean Salad, with a Shallot-Chardonnay Vinaigrette

FROM CHATEAU SOUVERAIN, GEYSERVILLE, CALIF.
GARY DANKO, CHEF

6 clusters of leaf lettuce

2 goat cheeses, 4 ounces each, sliced lengthwise into 3 pieces each

6 ounces petite green beans

3 tablespoons chopped shallots

assorted salad herbs: chopped chives, parsley, scallion slices, basil chiffonade (suit yourself as to amount)

DRESSING

1 cup chicken stock

½ cup Chardonnay

½ cup toasted walnuts shaken in a tea towel to remove skins

3 ounces walnut oil

3 ounces extra virgin olive oil

2 teaspoons Dijon mustard

2 teaspoons balsamic vinegar

salt and pepper to taste

Arrange salad greens on plate. Rub goat cheese with oil and place in oven-proof dish.

In stainless steel saucepan, reduce shallots, stock, and Chardonnay to 3 tablespoons. Cool slightly and whisk in mustard, vinegar, oils, salt, and pepper to balance. Add herbs.

Warm goat cheese at 350°F for 10 minutes. Sauté green beans in 1 tablespoon walnut oil until beans are light brown.

Divide beans among plates along with goat cheese, and spoon vinaigrette over top. Sprinkle with toasted walnuts.

Serves 6. (Suggested wine: Chardonnay.)

Warm Scallop Salad with
Basil Cream, Topped with Saffron Croutons

FROM CHATEAU SOUVERAIN, GEYSERVILLE, CALIF.
GARY DANKO, CHEF

6 clusters of leaf lettuce

1½ pounds scallops

scallion slices

4 tablespoons butter

DRESSING

½ cup Sauvignon Blanc

½ cup orange juice

2 cups fish fumet

3 cups heavy cream

12 medium basil leaves, chiffonade

parsley

CROUTONS

¼ cup olive oil

⅛ teaspoon saffron

French bread rounds

In nonreactive saucepan, simmer wine, juice, and fumet, and reduce over medium heat to 3 tablespoons. Add cream and reduce until sauce coats the back of a spoon. Salt and pepper to taste, and add basil and parsley.

Heat oil in a saucepan and add saffron. Remove from heat; brush bread rounds with the oil and bake until golden brown and crisp. Cut into bite-size cubes.

Arrange 6 plates with lettuce bases; place croutons atop salad.

In nonstick skillet, melt butter, quickly warm scallops through, and remove to salad. Add juices to cream base and season with salt and pepper. Correct sauce texture and spoon over salad. Sprinkle with scallions and serve promptly.

Serves 6 to 8. (Wine suggestion: Chateau Souverain Sauvignon Blanc, Sonoma County.)

Salad Greens
and Herbs

Garden Bouquet Salad
with Lemon-Herb Vinaigrette

FROM SHEPHERD'S GARDEN SEEDS, FELTON, CALIF.
RENEE SHEPHERD, PROPRIETOR

DRESSING

1 small green onion, chopped fine

1 teaspoon Dijon mustard

2 to 3 tablespoons lemon juice

1 tablespoon dry white wine

1 egg yolk

1 tablespoon minced parsley

1 tablespoon minced chive flower petals or chopped chive leaves

¼ teaspoon salt

pepper to taste

¾ cup extra virgin olive oil

With a whisk, combine all the ingredients except the oil. Slowly whisk oil in, beating continually until thoroughly blended. Taste for seasoning. Chill until ready to use.

SALAD INGREDIENTS

2 heads radicchio or red leaf lettuce

2 to 3 fresh sorrel leaves

2 small heads Bibb lettuce

12 to 14 leaves of young arugula or watercress

¾ cup fresh green and purple basil leaves

¼ cup borage flowers

Remove leaves from assorted vegetables; wash and dry. Reserve 6 to 8 radicchio or red lettuce leaves. Tear remaining radicchio, sorrel, lettuce and arugula into bite-size pieces and combine with basil leaves in center of salad bowl. Line outer edges with reserved radicchio or red lettuce leaves. Sprinkle with borage flowers around the outside border.

Whisk dressing and pour over the salad after presenting it at the table. *Serves 6.*

Memorable Wilted Lettuce Salad

FROM SHEPHERD'S GARDEN SEEDS, FELTON, CALIF.
RENEE SHEPHERD, PROPRIETOR

2 heads leaf or butterhead lettuce

DRESSING

8 slices very lean bacon, chopped

¼ cup vinegar

2 teaspoons water

2 teaspoons sugar

salt and pepper to taste

1 egg, beaten

Shred the lettuce into a large bowl.

Fry the bacon until crisp; don't drain the fat. Add the vinegar, water, sugar, salt, pepper, and beaten egg to the pan. Cook just until the mixture is thickened.

Pour the dressing over the lettuce and toss until the salad is wilted. Serve right away and stand back for applause.

Serves 6.

*Salad Greens
and Herbs*

Mixed Fresh Greens
with Curried Dressing

FROM SHEPHERD'S GARDEN SEEDS, FELTON, CALIF.
RENEE SHEPHERD, PROPRIETOR

1½ pounds assorted greens for 6 to 7 people

DRESSING

2 tablespoons white wine vinegar

1 tablespoon vermouth

1 scant tablespoon Dijon mustard

1 tablespoon soy sauce

¼ teaspoon ground cumin

½ teaspoon curry powder

1 teaspoon sugar

¼ teaspoon freshly ground pepper

⅓ cup salad oil

Wash, dry, and break greens into bite-size pieces.

Combine all dressing ingredients in a jar and shake well. Pour into salad bowl. Place greens in salad bowl on top of dressing but do not toss. Cover bowl tightly with plastic wrap and refrigerate for an hour or so.

Just before serving, toss after adding any or all of the following: 1 apple, diced; ⅓ cup dry roasted peanuts; ¼ cup golden raisins; 4 scallions, chopped; 1 tablespoon toasted sesame seeds.

Serves 6 to 7.

Vinaigrette for Salad Lovers

FROM SHEPHERD'S GARDEN SEEDS, FELTON, CALIF.
RENEE SHEPHERD, PROPRIETOR

¼ cup wine vinegar

1 to 2 teaspoons fresh lemon juice

½ teaspoon sugar

½ teaspoon mild prepared or Dijon mustard

2 to 3 teaspoons freshly chopped herbs (equal parts of basil, parsley,
thyme, and oregano, or equal parts basil, savory, and thyme, or equal
parts thyme, chives, and basil)

½ cup good light olive oil

1 clove garlic

Thoroughly blend all ingredients except garlic with a whisk or a fork. Let
the flavors blend at room temperature for an hour.

Rub the salad bowl with the freshly cut halves of the garlic clove. Add
washed and dried assorted crisp greens. Pour on the whisked-up dressing,
toss, and serve promptly.

Garden Greens with
Penne and Wild Mushrooms

FROM THE CHURCH STREET CAFE, LENOX, MASS.
CLAYTON HAMBRICK, CHEF-PROPRIETOR

1 pound penne or other tube pasta

¼ cup extra virgin olive oil

1 ½ cups roughly chopped shiitake or oyster mushrooms

1 ½ teaspoons minced garlic

½ teaspoon crushed red pepper flakes

4 cups chopped mixed greens to include: kale, radicchio, Belgian endive,
spinach, beet greens

½ cup chopped, cooked sun-dried tomatoes

6 ounces chicken stock, vegetable stock, or water

½ cup freshly grated Parmesan cheese

Bring salted water to boil and add pasta.

While pasta is cooking, heat the olive oil, then add garlic and mushrooms;
stir and sauté for 2 minutes, making sure garlic does not brown. Add pepper
flakes, greens, sun-dried tomatoes, and stock or water. Cook slowly for 3
to 4 minutes, and salt and pepper to taste.

Drain the pasta and toss with the greens. Sprinkle with grated cheese.
Serves 4 as entree, 8 as appetizer.

The Salad Lover's
GARDEN

6

Salad Crudités

Although crudités (raw vegetables) are technically finger food served hors d'oeuvres–style with dip, they have found their way into that great American institution known as "the salad bar." From there it was an easy leap into the family salad bowl. Crudités add a pleasing crunch to salads (tomatoes being the exception), add interesting colors and textures, and are higher in vitamins than cooked vegetables.

I've not listed peas, beans, potatoes, eggplant, cardoon, asparagus, and zucchini, among others, for lack of space, though all of these are fine salad makings when cooked and served chilled.

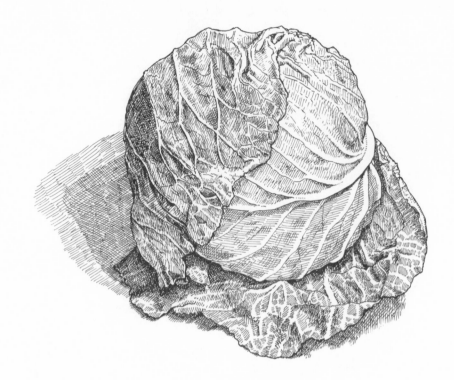

CABBAGE FAMILY

The vegetables I refer to here as the "cabbage family" are really part of a much larger and diverse group of plants known as the mustard family or Cruciferae. Its members include not just cabbage, cauliflower, and broccoli, but also Brussels sprouts, kale, collards, kohlrabi, mustard, rutabagas, turnips, radishes, and watercress (some of which are covered separately in this book).

Cabbage, of course, is the principal ingredient of coleslaw, which, by any standard, is a salad, simple as it is. Purple or red cabbage, with its sweet flavor and brilliant color, is very much at home in more stylish salads.

In recent years, raw broccoli and cauliflower, previously consigned to the buffet table surrounding a bowl of dip, have become prominent features of home salads. And so instructions for their culture are included here. Ornamental kale, picked when the leaves are young, has also made its way into American salads of late—because of both

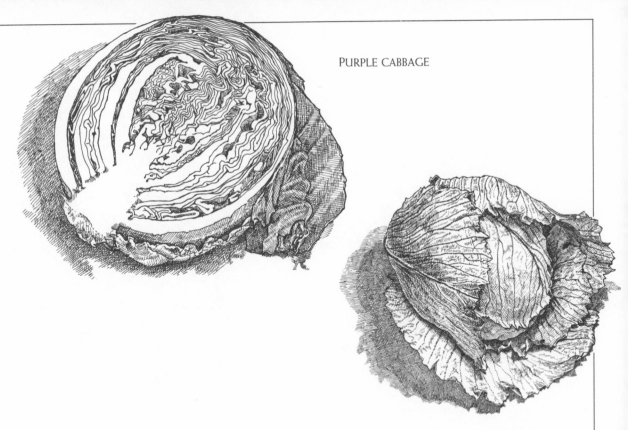

PURPLE CABBAGE

PURPLE CABBAGE

its tang and its color. For all their differences in appearance, these diverse members of the species *Brassica oleracea* have remarkably similar growing habits.

How to Grow Brassicas

Cabbage, broccoli, and cauliflower are cool-weather crops. The best way to get them off to a fast start is either to start seeds indoors six weeks before it's time to set out plants or to buy healthy nursery plants in the spring.

These crops do well in wide rows and raised beds, and they will even grow well together. Still, as they attract the same insect pests, it would be wise to plant them here and there around the garden in an effort to befuddle the marauders. Of course, that makes sense only

157

Salad Crudités

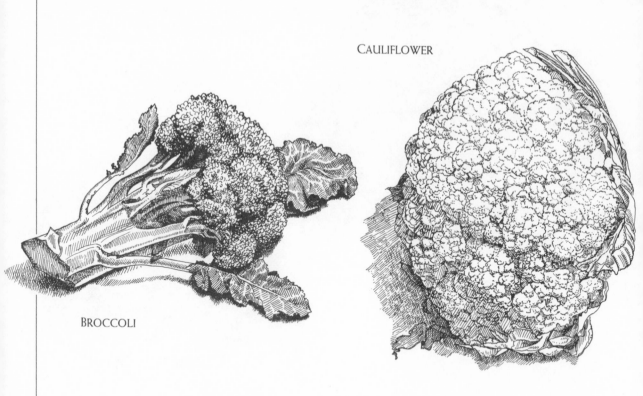

CAULIFLOWER

BROCCOLI

in a large garden. We'll discuss generally how to deal with cabbage pests a little later.

Plant brassicas in a staggered block pattern (see page 44): cabbage spaced 12 to 18 inches apart, broccoli and cauliflower 18 to 24 inches apart. Dig a planting hole 4 to 6 inches deep for each plant. Toss in a trowelful of compost and mix with a trowelful of soil. Strip off all but the top leaves and set each young plant into the soil right up to the top leaves. For protection against voracious cutworms, wrap a 2-inch strip of newspaper around each stem so that when the seedlings are set into their holes, an inch of the paper is above the soil line and an inch of it below. These collars are important—cutworms love the cabbage family. You must firm the soil around each plant very assertively; pack it down hard. This gives the stem the support it requires. Water gently but deeply. If cold, windy, or hot weather is predicted for the next several days, consider covering your young plants with hot caps or Reemay.

The Salad Lover's
GARDEN

How to Care for Brassicas

Once they've taken hold, brassicas grow quite swiftly, provided they are not set back by weeds or lack of water. So keep the water coming and, when heads start to form, topdress each plant with compost.

Another bit of help these plants enjoy is the added support offered when soil is hilled up around their stems as they grow. As you weed and cultivate with a hoe, take a moment to draw up a little extra soil around the plant stems. The additional soil not only provides support for these top-heavy vegetables but also insulates against loss of moisture.

In order to get perfectly milk-white heads of cauliflower, sunlight—which not only discolors the curds but reduces sweetness—must be kept off them. Plant breeders have developed self-blanching varieties, in which the outer leaves of the plant naturally curl over the young developing head to block the sun. But these leaves are never totally effective, and to properly blanch the heads will take a little extra time—plan on about five minutes or so per plant.

Blanching must begin when the head is no more than a couple of inches in diameter. The process involves bending or breaking some of the large outer leaves over the young head and tying them in place with string or large rubber bands. Remember, if you can see the head through the veil of leaves, then so can the sun. Check plants as the heads grow, and fold over additional leaves as necessary.

The greatest threat to brassicas comes from a couple of pests and diseases, but these will rarely do lethal damage in well-maintained soil. Cabbage loopers and cabbage worms are larve of the cabbage moth and cabbage butterfly; these larvae will eat their way through a stand of brassicas if not kept in check. The moths and butterflies lay their eggs on early crops just before the plants form heads. The larvae or "worms" hatch out soon after and gorge themselves on the leaves of their hosts. The best form of control is prevention—try to make your brassicas unattractive to the egg-laying parents. They are said to be repelled by strong aromas, so try interplanting with dill or onions or mint. (Take care with mint, as it will soon grow wildly out

159

RECOMMENDED VARIETIES
OF CABBAGE-FAMILY CROPS

Broccoli

• *Calabrese* In many ways this is the ideal salad broccoli, as the plant produces an abundance of small shoots ready to harvest at 3 to 4 inches long.

• *Emperor* Produces large, tight, and well-rounded heads of excellent flavor.

• *Premium Crop* Originally bred in Japan, these almost blue-green heads are especially delicious raw. Limited side shoots after main harvest.

• *Romanesco Minaret* Here's a special treat: a broccoli full of cone-headed florets of pale green. Flavor is sweet and mild.

• *White Sprouting* Like Calabrese; florets are white.

Cabbage

• *Early Jersey Wakefield* Probably the earliest of all cabbages and, therefore, the most desirable for salad gardeners. Pointy heads have delicious, sweet flavor.

• *Grenadier* This early variety produces medium-size heads that are truly delicious when thinly sliced in salads.

• *Salarite* Small, delicious heads with tender, semisavoyed leaves almost as mild as lettuce.

• *Scarlet O'Hara* A wonderful, early, deep burgundy colored cabbage that makes a pleasant salad addition for both its flavor and vivid color.

Cauliflower

• *Violet Queen* A purple cauliflower with broccoli-type florets! Delicious and good-looking in salads.

• *White Rock* An effectively self-blanching variety; pure white heads have terrific taste.

of hand. If you want to try it, I suggest planting it in small clay pots submerged throughout your brassica beds.) Homemade sprays of garlic, hot pepper, and soap, applied repeatedly, may also help deter the moths from laying eggs. And, of course, you can always cover the plants with Reemay.

If preventive measures don't work, the best controls include hand-picking (be sure to inspect leaves very closely, as the larvae are extremely well camouflaged) and the judicious use of *Bacillus thuringiensis* (Bt), a bacterium which when sprayed or dusted onto the leaves is deadly to the larvae. Try dusting leaves in the morning when they

The Salad Lover's
GARDEN

are still damp with dew. Other occasionally effective but less toxic dustings include rye flour, sifted wood ashes, lime, or table salt.

Clubroot, black rot, and blackleg are diseases which have never shown up in my gardens, but if your brassicas begin to blacken and yellow and wilt, they may have shown up in yours. Clubroot is a soilborne fungus disease encouraged by overly acid soil; a good liming before planting will help keep these spores dormant. Use varieties resistant to these diseases. As a preventive against blackleg and black rot, treating seed with hot water approximately 122°F is said to help. Otherwise, practice strict crop rotation, never planting brassicas in the same place for at least four years.

How to Harvest Brassicas

Harvest cabbage by cutting the head at the top of the stem with a good sharp knife. If you can cut the head so as to leave at least a pair of outer leaves growing on the stem, the plant will continue to produce small cabbage heads. Though these, in my experience, are never as tight or crisp as the first, main head, they are nonetheless excellent in salads.

Start harvesting cauliflower as soon as tight curds begin to form. Don't wait too long or the tiny flowers which form the curd will start to separate and become "ricey" and less flavorful. Once the head is harvested, you can uproot the plant, pulverize the fibrous and woody stems and roots with a shovel, spade, or hammer, and then deliver them to the compost pile.

As for broccoli, you can start your harvest of the central main head when it is 3 to 4 inches across. Don't uproot the plant, as it will continue to produce many perfectly tender and delicious single florets of up to 2 inches in diameter for weeks to come. Lazy as I am, I like these small florets better, for all they need by way of preparation is a vigorous rinse and a toss into the salad.

Other cabbage family crops to try are ornamental kales (both white and red types), collards, kohlrabi, broccoli di rapa, and Oriental crucifers such as Chinese cabbage, pakchoi, Chinese flat cabbage, and Abyssinian cabbage.

Salad Crudités

CABBAGE FAMILY AT A GLANCE

SOW INDOORS OR UNDER GLASS: 6 weeks before last expected frost.

GERMINATION: 7 to 10 days.

PLANT OUT: Early spring; can take light frost, but not a heavy freeze. Use cloches or floating row covers.

SEED DEPTH: ¼ inch.

DISTANCE BETWEEN PLANTS: 12 to 18 inches for cabbage (can be spaced closer for smaller heads); 18 to 24 inches for cauliflower and broccoli.

SOIL: Average; pH 6.0 to 6.8.

SUNLIGHT: Full sun.

WATER: Steady, moderate supply.

FEEDING: Topdress with compost or aged manure, and water with compost or manure tea when heads start to form.

COMPANION CROPS: Mint and other herbs, marigolds, onions.

CARROTS

Children tend to consider carrots *the* garden vegetable, but even for adults, carrots—thin orange wafers or shreds of them—will enliven any salad plate. As for taste, what compares with the sugary crunch of a sweet young carrot? Not much.

Though growing good carrots can be a little tricky, gardeners who've neither grown nor had success with them need not give up hope. In fact, if you give carrots the environment they require (which is not at all difficult to do), you'll get a good crop every time.

How to Grow Carrots

Your first consideration for truly excellent carrots must be the soil. Carrots will form long, slender, perfect roots in soil that is light, loose, well worked, and fairly rich. Heavy clay soil that compacts and cakes will retard germination at the outset, then hinder the downward, spherical growth of the roots, producing in the end a bent, forked, and otherwise misshapen crop. You also want to avoid soil that is stony or too rich in nitrogen for the same reasons.

How can you be sure of good soil for your carrots? As discussed previously, the principal course of action *over time* is the addition of organic matter to heavy soils for the purpose of fluffing them up. If your soil is really heavy, a more immediate tactic may be called for in the short run. Dig a trench about 8 inches deep and as wide as you'd like your carrot patch to be. Fill half the trench with clean builder's sand (available at building supply outlets) and the balance with a mixture of garden soil and compost or aged manure. Mix everything until it is well blended, then smooth the surface with the back of a rake. Wait a week for weeds to sprout, get rid of them, and start planting.

Carrot seeds take two to three weeks to germinate. To hasten germination, soak seeds for about an hour in a few tablespoons of strong, hot tea. Pour off the tea and scatter seeds on a paper towel until they have dried sufficiently to separate easily; the tiny carrot

CARROTS

Salad Crudités

seeds are difficult enough to handle without having to deal with them in wet globs.

I like to broadcast carrot seed in wide raised beds, and to make sure I get a more or less even distribution over the entire planting area I mix the seed in a bowl with a few handfuls of sand. Then I grab up pinches of the mixture and spread it as evenly as I can over the planting surface. Next, I cover the planting area with ¼ inch of sifted compost or light soil, then firm the soil surface with the back of a hoe or with my hand. I water with a mister if the soil is dry, and keep the seedbed moist until germination has taken place. For a steady supply of young roots, I sow a new crop every two weeks.

A word of caution: Never use fresh manure in your carrot bed, as it tends to create forked and fibrous roots.

How to Care for Carrots

The first thing you'll notice about your carrot crop is that it is over-crowded. And while that in itself can be solved by thinning, the very process of thinning creates another problem: It brings around the destructive carrot fly, which is attracted by the aroma emitted when carrot roots are bruised, which invariably happens during thinning. The carrot fly lays its eggs on the carrot root; when the larvae hatch out, they dig into the roots, and that's not the sort of ingredient you had in mind for the salad, believe me.

So when you thin, thin early and carefully until the maturing roots are standing 2 inches apart. Weed the carrot bed by hand to avoid damaging the roots. Also, interplanting carrots with garlic or onions helps to repel the carrot fly, and it makes for an interesting-looking bed.

If your soil is fairly rich, there is no need to sidedress your carrots during the season, although a light topdressing of compost never hurts. As for water, carrots appreciate a good, deep watering from time to time and never like dry conditions.

RECOMMENDED VARIETIES OF CARROTS

- *Gold Pak* This old standard produces wonderfully long, narrow, and tapering roots with excellent sweet flavor. It requires deep sandy soil to perform well.

- *Imperial Chantenay* Good flavor and orange color are features of this stocky, broad-shouldered, tapered root, which grows to about 4 inches. Good choice for heavy soils.

- *Little Finger* A gourmet baby carrot perfect for salads. Growing only 3 to 4 inches, this is an excellent choice for clay soils.

- *Minicor* Another baby carrot with fine flavor and color. Best harvested early. Good choice for heavy soils.

- *Parmex* An almost round carrot, this delicious variety with a diameter of up to 1½ inches is perfect for shallow and rocky soils.

- *Rondino* A long, tapered Nantes type, Rondino carrots are uniformly tapered roots, 7 inches long, with fine flavor and crispy texture. Best in deep or sandy soils.

- *Short 'n' Sweet* This short carrot (4 to 5 inches) has extremely sweet flavor and is well suited for heavy or shallow soils.

How to Harvest Carrots

Main-crop carrots are traditionally left in the ground until well into fall, at which time they are harvested for winter storage. Harvesting salad carrots, an activity likely to occur every couple of days, is very much like thinning and may well bring on the carrot fly if you're not careful. In loose soil, carrots will pull easily out of the ground, so grasp the green top about an inch above the root and pull. Generally speaking, the largest top will be growing above the largest root, so let size be your guide. Once a root has been pulled, cover over its hole with soil. And don't leave any traces of carrot root around to be scented by the carrot fly. Throw whatever you don't plan to use on the compost pile.

CARROTS AT A GLANCE

SOW INDOORS OR UNDER GLASS: Not an indoor starter.

GERMINATION: 14 to 21 days.

DIRECT-SEED OUTDOORS: As soon as ground can be worked. Sow every 2 to 3 weeks for continuous supply. Keep seedbed moist until germination occurs.

SEED DEPTH: ¼ to ½ inch.

DISTANCE BETWEEN PLANTS: 2 inches; keep thinning until proper spacing is achieved.

SOIL: Well-worked, light soil is ideal; use short or round-rooted varieties in heavier clay soils; pH 5.5 to 6.8.

SUNLIGHT: Full sun.

WATER: Moderate supply.

FEEDING: Not necessary in good soil.

COMPANION CROPS: Onions, peas, lettuce, and herbs (except dill, which is reputed to inhibit good root growth).

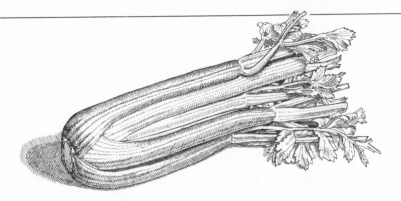

CELERY

A lot of people don't like celery in their salads, but I do from time to time. The challenge of growing celery has made it a few enemies along the way, for celery is a persnickety plant from first to last. It takes forever to germinate, requires just-so growing conditions for three months, demands special treatment in the form of blanching, and, in the end, lasts a precious few days in peak form once it is harvested. But if you like its crunchy presence in a salad, you might find celery worth a try.

How to Grow Celery

The secret of growing celery that has just the right combination of tenderness and cool crunch lies in the sort of rich, humusy soil that can hold water like a camel and at the same time promotes fast, unchecked plant growth. If that doesn't sound like your garden, and you still want to undertake the challenge of growing a few good stalks, you're going to have to bring in some reinforcements in the form of compost, leaf mold, and aged manure.

In other words, you're going to create a special growing situation for your celery. This will involve digging a trench to a depth of about 12 inches and as long and wide as the number of celery seedlings you want to plant. All this, mind you, must be done only after the threat of frost is past and when the soil has become pretty warm. Fill in half the trench with your mixture of organic material, and set out your homegrown or store-bought seedlings in straight rows, 12 inches

167

Salad Crudités

apart. Water them deeply and continue to do so if dry weather persists over the next week or two.

The young celery is now sitting in a trench about 6 inches below the surrounding soil. This makes a convenient water trough for these thirsty plants. In late summer, as celery starts the downhill run toward maturity, you will fill in the trench and, in so doing, "hill up" the plants for the purpose of blanching them. By keeping sunlight from all but the tops of the plants, blanching not only prevents the stalks from becoming dark but also sweetens and tenderizes the flesh. Cover as much of the plant as possible with soil, right up to the leaves, and pack it in good; but avoid getting more than a little into the plant's center or your celery may rot.

If you don't like dirty celery (and it will be dirty when you harvest it), you can still blanch the plants by staking wide boards on their edges along both sides of the row. Or you can cut off the tops and bottoms of half-gallon cardboard milk containers and slip one over each plant to accomplish the same end. In fact, anything you can devise that restricts light without restricting airflow will work.

There are self-blanching celery varieties which have a yellowish color and, as some gardeners feel, inferior flavor. Perhaps their palates are more refined than mine, but I enjoy the slightly blander taste of the self-blanching types as well as I do the standard varieties. Golden Self-Blanching produces pale stalks in 115 days. Tendercrisp is an early (105 days) and heavy producer.

Leaf miners, the offspring of the celery fly, are not uncommon. They bore into the leaves of the plant and make for unsightly-looking tops. Cut off any affected leaves with a sharp knife and remove them from the garden. An old-timer I used to know advised that mixing a shovel of chicken or cow manure in half a pail of water and then sprinkling the concoction on celery plants would keep the fly from laying her eggs there in the first place. Cheesecloth or Reemay over the plants will have the same effect. But if the flies get through, search for egg clusters and destroy them before they hatch. This will not be a difficult task with only a few plants. Also, practice crop rotation and keep weeds down—lamb's-quarters, for instance, is known to attract the celery fly.

How to Harvest Celery

Soon after celery is blanched, it should be harvested or you will face the possibility of the stalks drying out. Cut the plants at their base with a sharp knife. Late crops can be timed to coincide with the light frosts of early fall, which sweeten the flavor. Plants that are covered with cloches or heavily mulched with straw can survive well into late fall, even in Northern states.

CELERY AT A GLANCE

SOW INDOORS OR UNDER GLASS: 12 weeks before last expected frost.

GERMINATION: 14 to 21 days; thin seedlings to stand 2 inches apart in flats.

DIRECT-SEED OUTDOORS: Only in warm regions, as early as you can work the soil.

PLANT OUT: After last hard frost.

SEED DEPTH: $\frac{1}{16}$ inch; seeds are teeny, so barely press into soil.

DISTANCE BETWEEN PLANTS: 12 inches.

SOIL: Rich, well-worked, well-drained soil; pH 6.0 to 7.0.

SUNLIGHT: Full sun.

WATER: Steady supply; keep soil moist.

FEEDING: Topdress every two weeks with compost or aged manure, and water regularly with compost or manure tea.

CUCUMBERS

Though it perhaps reveals my unshakable provincialism, I must admit that a salad seems vaguely incomplete without a few thin slices of cucumber. Were you looking, you would invariably find two or three hills of cukes in my gardens: slicers, picklers, and, most recently, the long, slender, so-called "European" varieties. All make lovely additions to any salad, offering just the right sweetness and soft crunch we like from raw foods.

Growing cucumbers is remarkably easy. From seed to set fruit takes as little as six weeks. The trick in the salad garden with only limited ground space, however, is to manipulate the plant's normally extensive horizontal sprawl into vertical space. Train your cucumbers up a trellis or fence so that there is still room to grow the main ingredients of your salads. The other acceptable, though less challenging, option is to select the relatively new "bush" varieties over the standard vining cultivars. These types grow compactly, requiring only 3 feet of space between hills instead of the standard 6 to 8 feet, and produce cucumbers of excellent quality.

How to Grow Cucumbers

With a rake, mound up several hills of soil about 12 to 18 inches in diameter, 4 to 6 inches high; space them 6 feet apart for vining cucumbers and 3 feet apart for bush varieties. Scoop out the center of each hill and replace the soil with a shovelful of aged manure or compost and a topping of soil.

Using your finger, make a little circle on the top of the mound about 1 inch deep and plant about a half-dozen seeds, 2 inches or so apart. Cover the seeds, firm the soil around them, and water gently. When the seedlings emerge, thin to the strongest three, then cover each group with a plastic hot cap (which you can buy by the package in garden stores) or with a piece of floating row cover (see page 65), which is available in most seed and gardener supply catalogs. Plant protectors prevent sun and wind damage and keep insects at bay when the young plants are at their most vulnerable.

If you've grown seedlings indoors or bought some from a nursery (either is a good way to get an extra jump on the season), pop three of them out of their containers and plant them about 4 inches apart at the top of the mound. Firm the soil around each, water gently but deeply, and cover with plant protectors, as just described.

Cucumber trellises should be established on the north or east sides of the garden, where they will not cast unwanted shade on lower-growing plants. Unless, of course, a little shade is just what your midsummer lettuces are hungry for, in which case you should establish your trellis to their south during the dog days.

How to Care for Cucumbers

Cucumber vines will grow vertically to a height of 10 inches before starting their sprawl, which is also the time blossoms begin to appear. Some plants produce both male and female blossoms, and bees spread the fertilizing pollen from the male flowers to the females. Some cucumber varieties are gynoecious, meaning they have only female flowers and are self-fertilizing. You can tell a female blossom by the slight swelling beneath the flower itself. If you look closely, you will recognize this swelling as a cucumber-to-be.

In any case, when you first see blossoms, it is time to feed the plant. This is easily done by spreading a shovelful of manure or

171

Salad Crudités

Recommended Varieties
of Cucumbers

Long-Vine Types

- *Amira* A Middle Eastern hybrid of exceptional earliness, sweet flavor, and light green, smooth skin. Harvest at 5-inch size and yields will be heavy and continuous.

- *Burpless* Cukes are 9 inches long, extremely mild-flavored, and abundant. Climbs well on trellises and is disease-resistant.

- *Euro American* A hybrid of European greenhouse cukes and American slicers. Fruits are 9 to 10 inches long and exceptionally fine-flavored. Thick skin should be peeled for salads.

- *Marketmore* 80 Fruits are early and remain sweet even into the 8-to-9-inch size range. Plants seem less susceptible to attack from striped and spotted cucumber beetles and are disease-resistant.

- *Saladin* (pickler) An excellent gynoecious climbing variety; Saladin produces abundantly and early. Fruits are excellent as both picklers and slicers.

Bush Types

- *Northern Pickling* A high-yielding variety on 2-to-3-foot vines. Best picked at small size for uniformity of color and good pickler shape. Delicious for both salads and pickling.

- *Salad Bush* Full-size cucumbers on 2-foot vines have delicious flavor and relatively small seed cavity. Perfect for salad gardens.

- *Spacemaster* 7-inch fruits on 2-foot vines are extremely abundant. Excellent choice for small gardens and container plantings.

compost around the plants and watering it in. Or you can water regularly from this point of the season onward with a manure or compost tea.

How to Harvest Cucumbers

Like all fruiting crops, cucumber plants are made more productive by frequent harvesting. Simply put in botanical terms, plants want to perpetuate the species. They do so by setting blossoms, which develop into fruit, which produce mature seeds for future generations. Until a plant accomplishes its mission, it continues setting blossoms and fruit. But we cunning gardeners, armed with this information, snip off each fruit before the seeds are mature, which also happens to be when the fruit is best to eat, and so trick the plant into producing more and more.

So harvest your cukes regularly, and give yourself enough time to make a thorough search for those green devils hiding amid their thick and prickly leaves, so none get big and fat and yellow while they're on the vine. The best method of harvesting is to cut the stem with a sharp knife, leaving about a half inch of stem on each cuke.

CUCUMBERS AT A GLANCE

SOW INDOORS OR UNDER GLASS: 3 to 4 weeks before setting out for early crop; otherwise direct-seeding is fine. Sow seed in individual pots.

GERMINATION: 7 to 10 days.

DIRECT-SEED OUTDOORS OR PLANT OUT: When soil is warm and there is no longer any threat of frost. Cover plants with hot caps, cloches, or Reemay floating row covers.

SEED DEPTH: 1 inch.

DISTANCE BETWEEN PLANTS: 3 plants together in hills 3 to 6 feet apart, depending on variety.

SOIL: Rich, well fertilized; pH 6.0 to 7.0.

SUNLIGHT: Full sun.

WATER: Water deeply and often; keep upper 3 inches of soil moist.

FEEDING: Topdress with compost when blossoms appear.

COMPANION CROPS: Corn, radishes, marigolds, nasturtiums.

173

Salad Crudités

Onion Family

And, most dear actors, eat no onions nor garlic,

for we are to utter sweet breath;

and I do not doubt but to hear them say,

it is a sweet comedy.

—A Midsummer-Night's Dream

BULBING ONIONS

Thought in centuries past to be a cure for baldness (you rubbed onion juice "upon a pild or bald head in the Sun"), rabies, and the common cold, onions are a mainstay in any garden. Still, they inspire strange reactions from people. Some devotees of the most bitter chicories will demur at the sight of a ring of raw onion crowning the salad plate, while people who in all other things lean toward the bland will relish the hottest of the onion clan.

Onions in a salad—and you will see that there are many from the genus Allium which can be included—are intended to provide a zesty punch, an alternative to the sweet, buttery flavors of the lettuces. I've never been a great admirer of the fiery slicing onion (except in cooking, for which activity I generally put up about 50 pounds every fall), though in recent years I have come to appreciate the sweet Vidalia onion, a large-bulbing onion grown primarily in Southern gardens, and Walla Walla, its Northern counterpart. These I can eat with pleasure. Unfortunately, Vidalias do not store very well and must be used within two months of harvest or they start losing their crispness.

SCALLIONS OR GREEN ONIONS

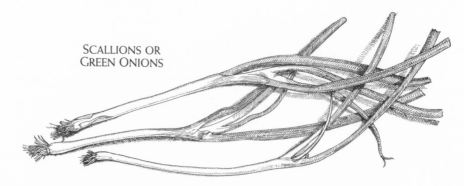

The Salad Lover's
GARDEN

Otherwise, I prefer to grow green onions, or scallions, for my salads, along with leeks, garlic, chives, and shallots. Additionally, there are the perennial Welsh onions and the weird but flavorful Egyptian onion, which bears its clove clumps both aloft on its stem ends and below the soil (when the stems topple and the bulblets growing there root and run).

How to Grow Onions

Onions, whether they are the slicing or the bunching (scallion) types, are best grown from seeds started under cover, for only in this way do you have the widest possible selection of interesting varieties. In late winter, sow the small black seeds in flats, and cover with ¼ inch of sifted planting mix (see page 59). Thin out dense clumps of the seedlings of bulbing varieties when they are 2 to 3 inches high, so they are ½ to 1 inch apart in the flat. They do quite well in what for other plants might be considered crowded conditions. Bunching onions can be sown and sustained in small clumps, 2 to 3 inches apart. If over time the tops get a bit leggy, shear them back with a scissors to a height of 2 inches and let them start growing again.

When transplanting into the garden—which you can do as early in spring as you can work the soil—first soak the flat so that intertwined plant roots will, with gentle pressure (*gentle*, mind you), pull apart without catastrophe. For economy of space as well as for benefits discussed in earlier chapters, onions should be planted in wide raised beds. Open shallow trenches 5 inches apart in the bed and set in your transplants about 1 inch deep. Fan out the roots as best you can. If the root hairs are scraggly, don't hesitate to trim them back a little with a sharp scissors.

If you have neither the facilities nor the ambition for indoor growing, but still want a good selection of onions, take heart. More and more gardening supply and seed catalogs are offering mail-order plants. In fact, this very season I ordered two bunches of Vidalias, having been unable to locate the seed in time.

Salad Crudités

And, finally, there is yet another time-honored way of planting onions, and that is by sets, immature onion bulblets grown the season before and kept dormant over the winter. These are available in white, yellow, and red varieties. Picked young as "green tails," they fulfill the function of scallions; left to mature until the tops die back, they'll produce creditable bulbs, with the yellow ones being generally good keepers.

SHALLOTS

Shallots are always started from sets; in fact, once you grow shallots for the first time, there is generally no need to buy these expensive sets in the future. A shallot planting invariably produces enough bulbs for a winter's supply in the kitchen, with enough left over to plant in next year's garden. After they are dried, place shallots in mesh bags and store in a cool space.

GARLIC

Garlic is also grown from sets, or, more accurately, from sections or "cloves" of the bulbs. The larger the set or the clove, the larger the crop will ultimately be. This is not necessarily the case with onions, where sets about ¾ inch in diameter are ideal.

To ensure that leeks will develop long, white, tender shanks, start them in trenches 4 inches deep, and as they grow, gradually fill in the trenches with compost. By the time the leeks reach maturity, they're fully blanched.

All the onions like rich, moist, well-worked soil and are best started in cool weather. True bunching onions—that is, onions whose bulbs never swell—can be grown quite close together, 1 to 2 inches apart. But bulbing onions must be thinned so plants have a good 4 to 5 inches to expand.

Bunching onions can be successively sown in the open garden every three to four weeks for a season's supply of this very pleasant addition to the salad bowl or crudité plate. Bulbing onions need the entire growing season to mature.

How to Care for Onions

LEEKS

When you're growing slicing onions, the truest sign of success is size. In fact, many a macho gardener stakes his reputation on just how big his bulbs are. Still, there are some tricks to it that are easy to master.

The first thing to remember is that onions are not a root crop, they're a leaf crop—the bulbs are formed by the plants' overlapping leaf bases. Onions don't do well if you try to grow the bulbs underground, something many a beginning gardener thinks is appropriate. With earth packed around them, the bulbs become restricted and simply won't grow very hefty, particularly when the soil is heavy.

Visualize an onion. Only its lower third wants to be in the soil. Any less and it will topple; any more and its growth will be restricted.

On the other hand, bunching onions or scallions don't form bulbs but are prized for their white bottoms as well as their green tops. You can increase the length of the white portion by hilling up the plants with soil. The portion of the stem that remains in the darkness will be blanched. The same is true for leeks.

177

Salad Crudités

RECOMMENDED VARIETIES OF ONIONS

Bulbing Onions

- *Copra* Medium-size, round onions, with good flavor. They are excellent keepers.

- *Sweet Sandwich* Mild-flavored, large onions that become sweeter and milder in storage. Good keeper.

- *Vidalia* Large, sweet, round onions with limited storage capability. Plants available through catalogs.

- *Walla Walla* Almost as sweet and mild as Vidalia, but Walla Walla onions keep well in storage for much of the year. Onions are large and somewhat flattened.

Bunching Onions

- *Evergreen Long White Bunching* Produces clusters of slender white stalks.

- *Red Beard* This Japanese scallion has a "wrapper leaf" that turns red in cool weather. Flavor is excellent, but bulbs will swell. Best planted as fall crop.

- *White Lisbon* Long white shafts that are crisp and sweet-flavored.

- *White Spear* One of the finest white bunching onions around. Long shafts are made longer by hilling, and the flavor will not overpower salads.

Keep all your onions well watered. Topdress with aged manure or compost once at scallion stage (when plants are 6 inches or so tall) and again when the bulbs start making growth. Keep the bed weeded and the plants properly spaced, and you'll have prizewinners.

If you are growing onions from sets, you may notice flower stalks emerging (they have tops that look like the peak of the Kremlin). Snip them off so the plant's energy can go to making bulbs, not seeds.

How to Harvest Onions

Scallions grown from sets can be harvested quite early, usually within three to four weeks of planting, when the plants are 6 to 8 inches tall; bunching onions grown from seed won't be ready for about two months.

Bulbing onions, shallots, and garlic are harvested when the tops turn brown and fall over. Pull bulbs on a warm and sunny day, which will allow them to dry a bit once they've been uprooted. I leave mine right on top of the bed for a few days, unless a long rainy spell is predicted. Let the bulbs dry outdoors until the roots become wiry and brittle. Once that happens, gather up your crop and bring it to a sheltered location that is open and airy, like a screened-in porch, for curing.

Cut the tops of the onions, leaving about ½ to ¾ inch of stem, and set the onions on an elevated screen if you have one, so air can circulate all around them. If you don't have such a screen, it doesn't matter; just turn the onions every few days so that they dry uniformly. Store them in mesh bags someplace where it stays cold but never freezes, such as an unheated attic or a dry, unheated basement.

ONIONS AT A GLANCE

SOW INDOORS OR UNDER GLASS: 8 to 10 weeks before setting out.

GERMINATION: 10 days.

DIRECT-SEED OUTDOORS OR PLANT OUT: As soon as soil can be worked.

PLANTING DEPTH: ¼ inch for seed; 1 inch for seedlings; bury sets up to their tips.

DISTANCE BETWEEN PLANTS: 4 inches for bulbing onions, shallots, and garlic; 1 to 2 inches for bunching onions.

SOIL: Rich, well drained; pH 6.0 to 6.8.

SUNLIGHT: Full sun.

WATER: Steady, heavy supply for expanding bulbs.

FEEDING: Topdress with compost twice during the season; water weekly with compost or manure tea.

COMPANION CROPS: Lettuce, carrots, peas.

PEPPERS

The array of pepper types available to gardeners these days is staggering. You'll find them in all colors (red, yellow, purple, orange, and of course green, which is the natural color of their immature stages) and shapes (blocky, bell-shaped, bonnet, and long and tapered).

Peppers are also classified as either "sweet" or "hot." I usually find the hot types a little *too* hot for inclusion in salads, because they can burn so intensely on the tongue that you barely taste the other ingredients. As a result, I stick pretty much to the sweet types.

How to Grow Peppers

Peppers, sweet or hot, are easy enough to grow—once you get them started. Pepper seeds can be a bit finicky about germinating if the soil temperature is substantially below 70°F. If you're starting plants indoors, try keeping the planting containers in a warm place until the seeds germinate.

Peppers do extremely well when sown in six-pack plastic cells or individual 2- or 3-inch pots. Sow two seeds per cell and snip off one with a scissors when plants develop their first set of true leaves.

Thereafter, grow the plants in cool temperatures, around 60° to 65°F. Seedlings will be ready for transplanting to the garden when they're about eight weeks old and when the last frost is a memory. Remember to harden off the seedlings very well before moving them to the garden. Set the transplants in planting holes about 2 inches deeper than they stood in their original containers. A tablespoon of garden sulphur mixed into the planting hole will help keep the pH at the desired level—unless your soil is already fairly acid.

How to Care for Peppers

You must follow two cardinal rules if you are to have a successful pepper crop. (1) Don't overfertilize the soil. Peppers require no nitrogen sidedressing if they're growing in good soil to begin with. When blossoms appear, however, you might try supplying them with necessary magnesium in the form of foliar spray—one tablespoon of Epsom salts to one quart of warm water. (2) Never let the soil dry out during the growing season. If rain is scarce, water by hand, especially after the plants have begun to set fruit. A heavy mulch will help conserve moisture.

Additionally, if your pepper-laden plants begin to teeter under the weight of their fruit, you can stake them to the very thin but sturdy bamboo supports used in flower gardens to keep tall flowers erect. As for pests, watch for slugs, flea beetles, and aphids. Select disease-resistant varieties whenever possible.

How to Harvest Peppers

When bell peppers become blocky and glossy, they are ready to eat. Hold the stem in one hand, and gently snap off the pepper with the other. Leave some fruit to turn color, which may or may not happen in short-season areas. Tapered peppers are best harvested when they begin to show color. When frost is forecast in late summer or early

Salad Crudités

Recommended Varieties
of Sweet Peppers

- *Corno Di Toro* These Italian peppers are red and yellow and resemble the bull's horn, for which they are named. Beautiful and flavorful in salads.

- *Early Prolific* Sets an abundant crop of medium-size blocky fruit even under difficult conditions.

- *New Ace* Good flavor and medium size for these peppers, which can set fruit in cool conditions. Well suited for Northeastern and coastal gardens.

- *Northstar* A good-size, husky pepper with three to four lobes. Flesh is thick, sweet, and crisp.

- *Purple Belle* Produces thick-walled, four-lobed peppers that are initially green, then become purple, and finally turn red when fully ripe. Compact plants are well suited for the salad garden.

- *Quadrato D'Oro* A Dutch variety of remarkable golden color. Flesh is thick, crisp, sweet, and aromatic. Disease-resistant.

- *Sweet Banana* Long, tapered peppers with thin walls that turn from light green to yellow, then to orange and red.

- *Sweet Chocolate* This unique brown pepper has sweet, thick, and crispy flesh. Bred in the Northeast, it also offers tolerance to cold weather.

fall, I pull up the entire plants and hang them upside down in the barn, where they stay cool and in good condition for a few additional weeks. If the weather turns warm again, as it sometimes does in my area of New England, I stand a chance of getting a good, colorful harvest—although, unfortunately, a more quickly deteriorating one.

See the box for recommended varieties of sweet peppers. If you want to grow hot peppers, try Anaheim, Long Red Cayenne, Early Jalapeno, or Hungarian Hot Wax.

The Salad Lover's
GARDEN

PEPPERS AT A GLANCE

SOW INDOORS OR UNDER GLASS: 6 to 8 weeks before last expected frost.

GERMINATION: 14 to 21 days.

PLANT OUT: After last frost. Set plants 2 inches deeper than they were in their last container.

SEED DEPTH: ¼ inch.

DISTANCE BETWEEN PLANTS: 12 to 18 inches.

SOIL: Moderately rich, well-drained soil; pH 5.5 to 6.8.

SUNLIGHT: Full sun.

WATER: Steady supply; keep soil moist, especially during fruiting period.

FEEDING: Spray 1 tablespoon of Epsom salts dissolved in a quart of warm water directly on leaves at blossoming time.

HARVEST: Wait until peppers are glossy and thick-walled; left on the plant, they'll eventually turn color.

COMPANION CROPS: Lettuce, marigolds.

Salad Crudités

RADISHES

Thin slices of radish in a salad offer a pleasing pungency. Radishes come in red, white, red and white, lavender, purple, yellow, and black, and they're all either round or cylindrical in shape. The craze these days is for a Japanese radish called Daikon, a crisp, finely textured, tapered radish that grows more than a foot long in the right soil and is every inch delicious. Considering the ease with which Daikon radishes grow, supermarket prices for them are outrageously high. The rarely seen long French radishes, equally easy to grow, are available in the more interesting seed catalogs.

If you're an impatient gardener, salad radishes are the crop for you. In as few as twenty days you can be eating these crunchy crucifers. Radishes are prone to split and turn fibrous not long after they reach a diameter of an inch or more, so plan on resowing small quantities every ten to fourteen days. Daikon matures in around fifty days and will last awhile; three separate sowings three to four weeks apart should keep you well supplied.

How to Grow Radishes

DAIKON RADISHES

Another of the excellent features of radishes is their ability to fit in anywhere. By virtue of their speed they are the ultimate catch crop; that is, they can be planted among a slower-growing crop (head

184

The Salad Lover's
GARDEN

lettuce, cabbage family crops, corn, tomatoes, peas, you name it) and will come to maturity and be harvested while the slow grower has barely reached adolescence. They therefore do not require their own patch of ground, unless, being the generous sort, you want to give it to them.

Work the soil especially well for Daikon and other long radishes. As with other root crops, avoid using fresh manure, which tends to produce forked and otherwise misshapen roots. Sow seeds in shallow drills among other, slower-growing plants, or broadcast them in their own patch. I usually mix radish and carrot seeds together; when the radishes are harvested, the carrots have additional room to grow to maturity. But no matter where you plant radish seeds, cover them with ¼ inch of sifted compost and firm them in place. Depending on weather conditions, the plants will be up in as few as five days. Thin the plants to stand about 1 to 2 inches apart once they've developed their first true leaves.

If you want to know what to do with your leftover radish seeds, sprout them as you would alfalfa or mung beans. The sprouts make a spicy addtion to salads or sandwiches. See page 192 for directions on growing your own sprouts.

How to Care for Radishes

The best radishes are those grown quickly, and to foster their rapid growth your primary responsibility in the brief period from germination to harvest is to keep the soil moist. Don't sidedress with nitrogen fertilizer, because the additional richness will result in big leafy tops and puny taproots.

Early radishes are up and out of the ground before insects can do much damage, but later crops can be affected by flea beetles and root maggots. Flea beetles are easily repelled with lime water or soap sprays frequently applied. According to John Seymour, author of *The Self-sufficient Gardener* (Doubleday, 1979), root maggots can be kept at bay by scattering small pieces of tar paper among the plants.

Salad Crudités

RECOMMENDED VARIETIES
OF RADISHES

Round Types

- *Champion* Bright red, round roots with a pungent radish flavor.

- *Cherry Belle* Mild-flavored, perfectly round roots with short tops. Extra early, yet retains flavor for several weeks.

- *Easter Egg* Lovely, mild-flavored radishes that produce in four colors: pink, purple, red, and white. Retains flavor even when roots become large.

- *Gala* This large radish is bright red and uniformly round. Flesh is crisp and mild. Good producer even in poor conditions.

- *Sparkler* A pretty radish, the Sparkler root is bicolored red and white, uniformly round, and small; best at about ¾-inch diameter.

Long Types

- *French Breakfast* Oblong-shaped root, 2 inches long, 1 inch in diameter. Skin is red with white bottom tips, and the crispy white flesh is moderately pungent.

- *French Golden* A pear-shaped, yellow-skinned root with fairly pungent white flesh.

- *Icicle* Tapered root, 4 to 5 inches long, with medium-hot flavor and crisp texture.

- *Mino Spring Cross (Daikon)* Long, tapered white radishes grow to lengths of 6 to 14 inches. Flavor holds up remarkably well—even into summer.

- *Omny (Daikon)* One of the best new hybrids available, producing slender white roots up to 16 inches long. Spring and fall crops.

How to Harvest Radishes

Pull 'em and eat 'em, and if the old crop is still in the ground when your first succession planting starts coming in, leave the old plants to run to seed. When the seedpods are young, harvest them for your salad. They are tender and delicious, especially those of the larger radish varieties, which are capable of producing an unexpectedly large number of pods.

The Salad Lover's
GARDEN

RADISHES AT A GLANCE

SOW INDOORS OR UNDER GLASS: Not an indoor starter.

GERMINATION: 5 to 10 days.

DIRECT-SEED OUTDOORS: As soon as soil can be worked.

SEED DEPTH: ¼ inch.

DISTANCE BETWEEN PLANTS: 1 inch.

SOIL: Light soil is ideal, but average soil will do; pH 6.0 to 7.0.

SUNLIGHT: Prefers full sun but will tolerate light shade.

WATER: Moderate—about 1 inch per week.

FEEDING: Unnecessary.

Salad Crudités

TOMATOES

Gerard's Herball tells us that the tomato's Latin designation, *Lycopersicon*—which derives from the roots for the words "wolf" and "peach"—is a perfect name since it alludes to both the beauty of the fruit and its danger. For quite some time, tomatoes were actually believed to be poisonous. Perhaps this old prejudice lingers still among certain connoisseurs who disdain the tomato as a salad ingredient, and who, when pushed, will only grudgingly accede to the presence of the cherry tomato among the greens. The principal sin of the tomato in the salad, according to these few, is that it invariably leaks a lot of water whether sliced or quartered, making the greens soggy and the dressing thin. The cherry tomato, included whole, obviously avoids the problem. So do quartered plum tomatoes, which are bred for meatiness and fewer seeds. But if you enjoy the taste of a luscious beefsteak and insist on having it in your salads, toss the greens and other ingredients separately and add the tomatoes only when the salad is already on your plate.

How to Grow Tomatoes

Tomatoes are simple to grow, whatever varieties you select. All types can be started indoors about six to eight weeks before the last expected spring frost, and set out in the garden when the soil has warmed up thoroughly. Or, naturally, you can buy seedlings at your local nursery. What you miss there, however, is selection—which may not be of great concern if all you want to grow is a half-dozen cherry tomato plants.

When you buy seeds, however, you have an almost unending array from which to make your selections. There are *determinate* or self-topping tomato varieties, which produce flower buds at the tips of their branches, thus limiting the plant's upward growth. *Small* and *strong determinate* varieties grow smaller and larger, respectively, than standard determinate plants. Finally, there are *indeterminate* types, which produce leaf buds at the branch tips and will continue to grow right up until frost. I grow determinate varieties in small wire cages, while the taller-growing indeterminates, of which cherry tomatoes are one, generally need tall stakes—about 6 to 8 feet.

Work the soil in your would-be tomato patch very deeply indeed, so the roots are free to expand. Double-dug raised beds are ideal. Dig your planting holes about 8 inches deep and 12 to 36 inches apart, depending upon whether plants will be staked, unstaked or caged. Toss a shovelful of compost or aged manure and a handful of bone meal into each, and mix in the bottom of the hole with regular garden soil.

Next, water the transplants and remove them from their containers, one at a time. Don't remove the next one until the first one has been planted, and you will spare them all needless stress. Strip off all but the top tuft of leaves from the plant, and set it into the hole so that the top leaves and an inch or two of stem are sticking out of the ground. Beginning gardeners are sometimes shocked by this denuding procedure, but they should be assured that the interred stem will send out feeder roots along its entire length, thereby strengthening the plant and increasing its ultimate productivity.

In any event, once the transplant is installed, firm the soil around the stem, driving out any possible air pockets, and water deeply.

Finally, if you plan to stake your tomatoes, drive the stakes into place now—generally on the side of the plant from which the season's prevailing winds come (which is the northwest in my corner of New England). This provides some safety for the plants; in a strong wind

Salad Crudités

RECOMMENDED VARIETIES
OF TOMATOES

Cherry and Container Tomatoes

- *Gold Nugget* To my way of thinking, the most delicious of all cherry tomatoes. Gold Nugget has rich yellow color, starts producing early, and continues its abundant production for months. Indeterminate.

- *Pixie Hybrid* Produces small crimson fruit about 2 inches across quite early. This cultivar is just right for patio containers. Determinate.

- *Principe Borghese* This Italian cherry tomato is grown primarily for sun drying. Does well in arid climates. Indeterminate.

- *Sweet 100* Another favorite of mine, this variety produces hundreds of very sweet cherry tomatoes over a long season. Indeterminate.

- *Tiny Tim* An old standby, these dwarf plants produce abundantly beginning early on. Excellent for containers. Determinate.

Pear or Plum Tomatoes

- *Milano* This extremely early pear-shaped tomato, with its small seed cavities, is fine for salads. Yields are prolific on short, compact plants. Determinate.

- *Roma VF* Produces large plum-type tomatoes on compact vines. Determinate.

Main-Crop Determinate Varieties

- *Johnny's 361* This beefsteak type produces red 8-ounce fruits that have excellent flavor as well as disease and crack resistance. Best of all for salad gardeners, it requires only limited space.

- *Marmande* This early variety is a French heirloom. Plants produce large, round, red fruits even in cool climates. Semideterminate.

Main-Crop Indeterminate Varieties

- *Better Boy* A large-fruited variety, Better Boy has the advantage of producing lots of foliage to protect tomatoes against sunscald. Flavor is fine and plants are resistant to nematodes.

- *Bonny Best* This old-time favorite produces delicious red fruit up to a half pound.

- *Burpee's Big Boy* Uniformly round, smooth fruits up to a pound with thick, sweet tomato flavor. Disease-resistant.

- *Firebird* A beautiful pink staking tomato with delightful flavor; adds a lovely aesthetic touch to any salad.

they will not be driven by gusts against their stakes, but rather will be pulling away from them. Cages should also be set in place at this time, to avoid damage to spreading roots later on.

Another tomato-planting technique I learned years ago when working with master gardener Dick Raymond calls for digging a shallow planting trench 3 to 4 inches deep and a little longer than the length of your tomato plant. Strip off all but the top leaves and lay the plant on its side in the trench, cradling the top leaves in one hand while covering the stem and roots with the other. Set your stake an inch or two from the exposed stem. In a week or so, the supine top will begin to grow straight up, and not long after you'll be able to hitch it to the stake.

Dick maintained that the stem, lying horizontally in the ground, would create a more massive root system than a stem of equal length buried vertically. He also felt that because the trench was shallower, the roots, being closer to the surface, would receive more heat. And right he is, except that moisture evaporation is greater nearer the surface, and plants must therefore be watered more frequently. I'd not take this route if I lived in an area of limited rainfall.

How to Care for Tomatoes

Gardeners often test their mettle by the date of their first ripe tomato. Being heat lovers, young tomato plants will respond to added warmth by growing, setting blossoms, and ripening fruit quickly. To create warmer conditions for their tomatoes, gardeners create miniature greenhouses for individual tomato plants with such devices as plastic milk jugs, large hot caps of clear plastic, and heat-releasing devices called Walls-o'-Water, which are available in garden centers and from mail-order suppliers for a few dollars each. Another simple but effective way to bring heat to young plants is to cover the ground in which they're growing with something black—like black plastic sheeting. The black materials absorb heat and suppress weeds.

Keep the water coming during the early growing period, but when the plants set fruit, give them less water. At this time, topdress

Salad Crudités

SPROUTING SEEDS

Producing one's own sprouts is a form of indoor gardening few salad lovers undertake, preferring instead to buy small boxes of sprouts at the greengrocer's. Buying sprouts is all well and good, except that, unless you eat them quickly, their flavor and nutritional value go downhill and they get gooey with top rot. A better idea is to sprout your own in small quantities for a steady supply of these ultimate seedling crops.

Seeds to Use

Many types of seeds can be used for home sprouting, and most of them are available at health-food stores. You might try sprouting alfalfa, radish, mung bean, adzuki bean, lentil, kale, broccoli, cabbage, cauliflower, buckwheat, and wheat. If your health-food store doesn't carry all of these seeds, the proprietor should be able to tell you who does.

How to Sprout Seeds

You can buy inexpensive seed-sprouting kits which come with their own instructions, or you can go it alone. Under the right conditions, most seeds will sprout in as little as two days and no more than a week. Here's how to do it:

1. Rinse the seeds. Cover them with cold water and allow them to soak overnight. Pour off the water in the morning and rinse seeds again.

2. Once the seeds are drained, place them in a shallow bowl or dish, about 2 inches deep, in a layer no deeper than ½ inch or so. Cover and place the dish in a warm spot where the temperature will be consistently about 70°F—in the light or in darkness.

3. For the next few days, rinse the seeds morning and night with fresh, cool water. This is *vital*. Drain well before returning seeds to dish. Using a screen cover on the bowl makes rinsing easy.

4. When sprouts are ready to eat, refrigerate them and rinse them once a day to prolong freshness.

or sidedress with aged manure or compost, then mulch the plants with straw or grass clippings to help retain steady moisture.

To keep staked indeterminate tomato plants from becoming unmanageable, you can prune or "sucker" them regularly right through the season, removing all but a couple of the leafy shoots or "suckers" that grow in between the main stem and the side branches. When the plants begin to outgrow their stakes, pinch off the bud at the top of the two or three main stems, and the plants will cease their vertical growth. Some gardeners with plenty of open space let their tomato plants sprawl, unsupported, on mulched ground, in which case suck-

The Salad Lover's GARDEN

ering is unnecessary. In wet seasons, slugs and disease can be a problem for unstaked tomatoes.

Pests that make their livings on tomato plants are many, including flea beetles, Colorado potato beetles, tomato hornworms, and fruit-worms. There are also a number of common diseases, identified by the symptoms they produce: wilt, mosaic, blight, and blossom-end rot. Home-brewed soap sprays or lime water will keep flea beetles away; handpicking or dusting with Bt (see page 55) will check the rest. For disease control, choose resistant varieties, and where disease has been a problem in the past, avoid growing tomatoes for a good three or four years. If your garden is so small that this last measure is impossible, I suggest that you grow your tomatoes in suitable containers outside the garden, using uncontaminated soil. There are small-fruited tomatoes especially suited to container growing.

TOMATOES AT A GLANCE

SOW INDOORS OR UNDER GLASS: 6 to 8 weeks before last frost.

GERMINATION: 7 to 10 days.

DIRECT-SEED OUTDOORS: Only in warm climates.

PLANT OUT: When ground is warm; cover plants with heat conservers such as hot caps, cloches, Walls-o'-Water.

SEED DEPTH: ¼ inch.

DISTANCE BETWEEN PLANTS: Staked, 12 to 18 inches in rows 3 feet apart; unstaked, 18 to 24 inches in rows 4 feet apart; caged, 24 to 36 inches in rows 4 feet apart.

SOIL: Rich, deep; pH 5.5 to 7.5.

SUNLIGHT: Full sun.

WATER: Steady, moderate supply; avoid overwatering as fruits start to enlarge.

FEEDING: Topdress when blossoms appear and weekly thereafter; water with manure or compost tea.

COMPANION CROPS: Onions, garlic, marigolds, parsley, basil.

Appendix:
Suppliers of Seeds
and Gardening Accessories

Burgess Seed & Plant Company
905 Four Seasons Road
Bloomington, IL 61701

W. Atlee Burpee Co.
300 Park Avenue
Warminster, PA 18974

Comstock, Ferre & Co.
263 Main Street
Wethersfield, CT 06109

The Cook's Garden
Box 65
Londonderry, VT 05148

Joseph Harris Co.
3670 Buffalo Road
Rochester, NY 14624

Heirloom Gardens
P.O. Box 138
Guerneville, CA 95446

Herb Gathering Catalog
4000 West 126th Street
Leawood, KS 66209

High Altitude Gardens
P.O. Box 4238
Ketchum, ID 83340

Le Jardin du Gourmet
West Danville, VT 05873

J. L. Hudson, Seedsman
P.O. Box 1058
Redwood City, CA 95446

Johnny's Selected Seeds
Albion, ME 04910

Le Marche Seeds International
P.O. Box 566
Dixon, CA 95620

Mellinger's Inc.
2310 West South Range
North Lima, OH 44452

Nichols Garden Nursery
1190 North Pacific Highway
Albany, OR 97321

George W. Park Seed Co.
P.O. Box 31
Greenwood, SC 29646

Pinetree Garden Seeds
New Gloucester, ME 04260

Richters Herb Catalog
Box 26
Goodwood, Ontario
Canada L0X 1A0

Seeds Blum
Idaho City Stage
Boise, ID 83707

Shepherd's Garden Seeds
6116 Highway 9
Felton, CA 95018

Stokes Seeds Inc.
737 Main Street, Box 548
Buffalo, NY 14240

Thompson & Morgan
P.O. Box 1308
Jackson, NJ 08527

The Tomato Seed Company
P.O. Box 323
Metuchen, NJ 08840

Vermont Bean Seed Company
Garden Lane
Bomoseen, VT 05732

SOURCES OF EQUIPMENT AND SUPPLIES

Bountiful Gardens
Ecology Action
5798 Ridgewood Road
Willits, CA 95490

Gardener's Supply Catalog
128 Intervale Road
Burlington, VT 05401

Gardens Alive!
Natural Gardening Research Center
Highway 48, P.O. Box 149
Sunman, IN 47041

Langenbach Garden Tools
P.O. Box 454
Blairstown, NJ 07825

The Necessary Catalogue
Necessary Trading Company
P.O. Box 305
New Castle, VA 24127

Ohio Earth Food, Inc.
13737 Duquette Avenue N.E.
Hartsville, OH 44632

Smith & Hawken
25 Corte Madera
Mill Valley, CA 94941

The Salad Lover's
GARDEN

Index

Index